TWENTIETH CENTURY INTERPRETATIONS

OF

BLEAK HOUSE

TWENTIETH CENTURY INTERPRETATIONS
OF

BLEAK HOUSE

A Collection of Critical Essays

Edited by
JACOB KORG

Prentice-Hall, Inc. A SPECTRUM BOOK *Englewood Cliffs, N. J.*

Copyright © 1968 by Prentice-Hall, Inc., Englewood Cliffs, New Jersey. A
SPECTRUM BOOK. All rights reserved. No part of this book may be reproduced
in any form or by any means without permission in writing from the publisher.
Library of Congress Catalog Card Number 69–11357. Printed in the United States
of America.

Current printing (last number):

10 9 8 7 6 5 4 3 2 1

Prentice-Hall International, Inc. (*London*)

Editor's Note

For the sake of uniformity, all references to *Bleak House* have been regularized and appear as chapter references in Roman numerals. The critics represented here have used various editions of the novel. The favored one is volume 13 of the *New Oxford Illustrated Dickens* (London, 1948, reprinted 1956).

For assistance in preparing this volume, I should like to acknowledge my indebtedness to Richard J. Dunn, Paul Hunter, and Julian Reid.

Contents

TWENTIETH CENTURY INTERPRETATIONS

OF

BLEAK HOUSE

Introduction

by Jacob Korg

Although *Bleak House* has deeply engaged the attention of modern critics, it was not a favorite among Dickens' contemporaries. It attracted great attention and gained a wide circulation because it was a new work by the most popular novelist of Victorian England, whose last novel, *David Copperfield*, had raised his fame to higher levels. *Bleak House* was published in 1852–53 in the format usual for Dickens' novels, the monthly shilling serial that presupposed the existence of a huge public which would be willing to follow the story for many months. It sold even better than *David Copperfield*, rising to a monthly distribution of 35,000 copies in comparison with the earlier novel's 25,000. In spite of this success, however, there was much adverse comment. A number of interests were offended by the novel's social criticism. Proponents of government, the law, philanthropy, and feminism felt that Dickens had been unfair to their causes, and that he had ignorantly stirred up skepticism about them. There were protests against the grotesqueness of such figures as Krook and Smallweed, who were, as Dickens' biographer John Forster wrote, "much too real to be pleasant." Many people knew that Dickens had satirized his friend, Leigh Hunt, in the figure of Harold Skimpole, and they objected to this cruelty. Contemporary reviewers conceded that *Bleak House* contained some of the best things Dickens had ever done in his familiar style, and they praised the complexity and tightness of the plot. The character of Jo was widely admired, less as an instance of social injustice than as a figure of pathos and sentiment. But it was generally complained that Dickens' new novel too often offered satire instead of humor, complexity instead of vividness, and artifice instead of spontaneity, and that his feeling about the poor had been transformed from an edifying sympathy to a disturbing and vindictive indignation. *Bleak House*, it was said, lacked the innocence, geniality, generosity, and warmth that Dickens' readers had associated with his name since the success of his first novel, *Pickwick Papers*, sixteen years before.

The complex of qualities that had made Dickens the leading novelist of his time, and an author who enjoyed a unique intimacy with an immense and varied public, is not easily formulated. He had begun his writing career as a reporter, working under conditions that demanded accuracy, fluency, and energy; and the journalistic environment in which he wrote his first short fictional and descriptive pieces trained him to think in terms of the needs and interests of his readers. But he was also a self-expressive artist of strong romantic tendencies, whose ultimate sources of power lay deeply buried in his emotions. *Bleak House* contains many of the elements that had made Dickens popular; it has vivid narrative, comedy, swift action, and the detailed, affectionate treatment of character and setting that had always entertained his readers; and it also contains the pathos, terror, violence, and sense of social injustice that had moved them.

Bleak House is less autobiographical than *David Copperfield* or *Great Expectations,* but only because its connections with Dickens' private life are less direct. One of his strongest feelings about himself is expressed through the figures of Jo, Charley, and Esther, varied renderings of the familiar Dickensian theme of the neglected child. As a boy of eleven or twelve, after his family had moved to London in what the Victorians described as "reduced circumstances," Dickens was put to work in a factory that manufactured shoe-blacking. The work was not hard, but the bright and ambitious little boy felt shamed and degraded by it. In a memoir of his childhood that became known only after his death, Dickens reported that he felt he had been "thrown away," that he had been consigned to a meaningless, drudging existence without the chance of an education.[1] At the same time, his father was imprisoned for debt, and the boy's isolation and despondency increased as he was left to wander the streets and make the most of his small earnings. This short period of Dickens' life had a disproportionately profound effect on his writing. In particular, it generated his heartfelt treatment of the many orphans and stray children of his novels, and gave him memories to be used in the scenes of prison life found in *Pickwick Papers* and *Little Dorrit.*

When his father, after coming into a small inheritance, was released from prison, Dickens went to a conventional school for a couple of years, and then, at the age of sixteen, entered a lawyer's office as a clerk. This was the first of his many opportunities to observe the legal

[1] Dickens' autobiographical account is quoted in John Forster's *Life of Charles Dickens* (London: Chapman and Hall, Ltd.), I, 24–35.

profession, a subject which is one of the great strengths of his novels. He gathered impressions of the law in action a little later when, after following his father's example and learning the difficult art of short-hand writing in order to qualify himself as a recorder of Parliamentary speeches, he spent the time waiting for an appointment to the group of Parliamentary reporters by doing this work in courtrooms. He was said to have taken down the proceedings in Lincoln's Inn Hall, the fog-bound chamber that is the scene of Jarndyce and Jarndyce, but worked for the most part in the courtroom known as Doctors' Commons. The proceedings here were generally dull; the cases were mainly matrimonial or ecclesiastical disputes, many of them trivial, and no doubt verging on the comic. But for two years Dickens observed the behavior of barristers and their clients, and recorded the absurdity, pathos, and tedium of the cases. During his clerkship and his period in Doctors' Commons, Dickens worked with young men like Guppy and Small-weed, and had lawyers like Kenge, Vholes, and Tulkinghorn as his employers. This experience became the basis of his thorough knowledge of the life of the legal profession, in all its levels and gradations of activity, that is so conspicuous in many of his novels, especially in *Bleak House*.

Dickens left law-reporting and took the very responsible position of Parliamentary shorthand recorder at the age of nineteen. The super-sensitive and forlornly genteel twelve-year-old of the blacking ware-house had somehow turned into an ambitious, lively, and supremely competent young man. London now became a field for exploration and observation rather than a wilderness, and this period of Dickens' young manhood had as much to do with his work as a novelist as any other. He was able to draw upon his experience of London streets and people with sure effect in describing Tom-all-Alone's and its inhabitants, the nighttime city seen during the pursuit of Lady Dedlock, and such Holborn locales as the cemetery and the court where Snagsby's shop is situated.

He also frequented the theater, and had ambitions of becoming an actor; this lifelong interest is of vital importance in his work, for, as Mr. Garis shows, his approach to narration is often dramatic and his gift for presenting striking characters like Krook, Miss Flite, and Mr. Chadband depends on an imaginative identification allied to acting. His work as a reporter sent him to various provincial towns to cover elections and record speeches; these trips gave him a wide knowledge of England and of the hazards and discomforts of travel at a time when coaches were the best means of transportation. Dickens never ceased to regard travel, whether by coach or train, as an adventure, and this sense of his has much to do with the excitement of Bucket's and Esther's pursuit of Lady Dedlock.

Dickens' work as a novelist originated in journalism. He did his first imaginative writing for pleasure. In 1832 and 1833, while he was working as a shorthand reporter in the House of Commons, he sent a number of lively little stories and descriptions to a periodical called the *Monthly Magazine,* which published them without pay. In 1834, he contributed similar pieces to the newspaper he worked for, the *Morning Chronicle,* and in the following year wrote a series of them for a related publication, the *Evening Chronicle,* this time earning something for them. These stories were published in 1836 in two volumes under the title *Sketches by Boz,* and a publisher who read them decided to ask Dickens to undertake the project that was to become *Pickwick Papers.* This first novel was immensely popular, and made Dickens famous. Before long he married, gave up his reporter's job, and plunged with terrific momentum into a career as a writer. Before *Pickwick* had completed its run of monthly issues, Dickens found himself writing two novels simultaneously, editing a newly founded magazine, doing odd jobs of writing and editing, and committing himself to write further novels.

Pickwick Papers was a comic masterpiece; but instead of repeating this presumably safe victory, Dickens undertook, in his second novel, *Oliver Twist,* to tell a story of adventure, sentiment, crime, and social protest. His public learned that its new favorite was not merely a humorist, but had an impressive range, which was to expand and augment itself constantly, in book after book, as Dickens rose to become a universally known public figure. He was no Olympian; he was immersed in the life of his time as a writer and editor of periodicals, an advocate of social reforms, an active philanthropist, and, in his readings and speeches, a performer who often faced large audiences with triumphant effectiveness.

During the fifteen years after *Pickwick Papers,* Dickens not only wrote the series of great novels leading up to *Bleak House,* but carried on extensive editorial work and made long trips to the United States and Italy, writing a book of travel notes about each of these journeys. Each of the novels written during this time was a compound of various effects and appeals; Dickens found room in them for social satire, effects of Gothic terror, powerful accounts of crime and poverty, dramas of sin and its consequences, and criticism of social follies and extremes. But his public looked to him particularly for his incomparable humor, warm sentimentality and pathos, and exciting or amusing stories enacted by vivid characters. For the uncritical majority of his readers, a Dickens novel was an experience of laughter, tears, suspense, and a final emphatic confirmation of the conventional attitudes toward love, marriage, family life, and philanthropic obligations. With *David Copperfield* he came closer than ever to his audience by appealing, from the firm ground of his own experience, to the reader's taste for the comic and sentimental through the intimate tone of a first-person narrative.

In *Bleak House*, however, Dickens undertook to fulfill responsibilities that had been more or less ignored in *David Copperfield*: responsibilities toward form, coherence, plot organization, and particularly toward issues of public morality. For one thing, he commented even more vigorously and incisively than before on some of the serious social questions of the day.[2] The problem of poverty represented by Jo, the brickmakers, and Tom-all-Alone's was, of course, one of the most persistent central themes of Victorian social thought, and while Dickens was already famous as an eloquent advocate of the poor, *Bleak House* is one of his most powerful protests on the subject. The excesses of the Court of Chancery, long an occasional subject of Dickens' criticism, were particularly prominent in 1851, for Parliament was considering a Chancery reform bill through most of the year and actually passed such a measure just before Dickens began his work on *Bleak House*. The case of Jarndyce and Jarndyce is based on an actual suit, the famous Jennings case, which concerned a fortune left by a miser who had died in 1798 without leaving a will, and which was still unsettled in 1915. Dickens' treatment of Chancery illustrated the two-way relationship which could exist between a serial novelist and his readers, for after a few numbers of *Bleak House* had appeared, a reader sent Dickens a pamphlet which told the history of a Chancery suit about a Staffordshire farm, and Dickens used some of these details in his account of Gridley's case. Having seen Parliament at first hand during his days as a reporter, he was often bitterly critical of it, and the Parliamentary indecision discussed at Chesney Wold may well be

---

[2] For details, see John Butt and Kathleen Tillotson, *Dickens at Work* (London: Methuen & Co. Ltd., 1957), Ch. VII, "The Topicality of Bleak House." For comments on the historicity of *Bleak House*, see Humphry House, *The Dickens World* (London: Oxford University Press, 1941), pp. 30–33.

an allusion to a then-recent period of exceptional instability in the
government. The satire on "telescopic philanthropy" embodied in
Mrs. Jellyby may have referred to an ill-fated expedition mounted
about ten years before by the African Civilization and Niger Association; but the scene in which Jo eats his pauper's breakfast on the steps
of the Society for the Propagation of the Gospel in Foreign Parts is a
thrust at an institution active at that time. Philanthropists of varied
persuasions were incensed by the satire of *Bleak House*; one critic said
that the characterization of Mrs. Jellyby was an attack upon people
who were working to abolish slavery; and by having her take up the
cause of the rights of women at the end of the novel, Dickens antago-
nized feminists as well.

It is, therefore, not surprising that *Bleak House* should have aroused
controversy; but it is now also clear that it inaugurated a period in
Dickens' career in which his earlier optimism was overshadowed by a
serious attitude arising from a more mature and sensitive view of
moral problems. This new and gloomier manner was regarded by
many as a falling-off, but Dickens was too well established for his
popularity to suffer. The sales of *Little Dorrit* equalled those of *Bleak
House*; *Hard Times* and *Great Expectations*, uncompromisingly serious treatments of the theme of moral responsibility, bolstered the
success of the magazines in which they appeared as weekly serials.
Beginning in 1853, Dickens capitalized further on his fame by giving
public readings from his novels, and this made it possible for large
audiences to hear and see the man whose work they had been reading
eagerly for many years. Even the news that he had been separated from
his wife in 1858, which seriously damaged his public image, did not
interfere with his popularity. In 1867–68, he returned to the United
States, where he was as well known as in England, to give a long series
of readings. These performances were profitable but arduous. He con-
tinued to write and to give readings for a time after returning to
England, but he felt the effects of the American tour until his death
in June, 1870.

In *Bleak House*, Dickens' energies function in two distinct ways.
His prodigious inventive power extends itself, in its familiar manner,
into constantly expanding reaches of action and incident, minting
vivid new characters and settings and devising vigorous ramifications
of the plot. But an equally creative counter-pressure is brought to
bear on these elements to establish their relationships with one another
and their relevance to the moral issues at the center of the novel. This

organizing discipline appears in an earlier novel, *Dombey and Son,* where Dickens made a special effort to adhere to the requirements of his plot and theme; it was set aside, appropriately enough, for the autobiographical *David Copperfield.* But Dickens took it up again in *Bleak House,* carefully shaping the sprawling materials of his story in a variety of ways, so that the art of the particular, in which he is always masterful, is brought into balance with the art of relationship. "The final impression," says W. J. Harvey, "is one of immense and potentially anarchic energy being brought—but only just—under control." [3]

The plot of *Bleak House* is as sensational and coincidence-ridden as any in Dickens' novels. It is neither an exposition of subtle causalities nor a tracing of the "stealthy convergence of human lots" that George Eliot mentioned as a feature of the provincial scene she described in *Middlemarch.* The baroque implausibilities of *Bleak House* convey a different sense of life, a fierce conviction, often toned with despair, that no deed is without its consequences. In the first half of the story, to be sure, the plot makes few claims of this kind. The developments leading to the discovery of Hawdon's identity, and those of his wife and daughter, occur at widely separated intervals and in almost casual fashion, like the sluggish heartbeats of a hibernating animal. It is not at all clear that the fragmentary clues turned up by the different investigators belong to a single structure of events. But when the different paths of discovery converge at the death of Tulkinghorn, the whole complex of past and present actions springs to life, in spite of its artificiality, because it is animated by the root idea that the present can be threatened by the moral burdens imposed by the past.

The action is not well unified; the separate interests of the Chancery suit and Lady Dedlock's crime spin around different centers and touch only incidentally. They are related to each other, in a mode which outflanks plot considerations altogether, as parallels; in each of them a powerful force is seen moving irresistibly to crush the human beings who stand in its path. But the linking of apparently unconnected characters and episodes within each of the sub-plots, sometimes through the most trivial details, dramatizes the authentic relationships that exist among them. It also embodies one of the principles to which the

[3] "Chance and Design in Bleak House," in *Dickens and the Twentieth Century,* eds. John Gross and Gabriel Pearson (London: Routledge & Kegan Paul Ltd., 1962), p. 146.

novel, as a genre, is committed, the principle that within a social
context even the most ordinary incidents can acquire overwhelming
power and significance. Lady Dedlock's momentary slip, betraying
her familiarity with the handwriting of a legal paper, generates a
sequence of events that reaches far back into her shameful past and
branches out to touch the furthest reaches of the novel. It motivates
Tulkinghorn's investigation, which leads to the involvement of Jo in
Esther's life, and also, by making Tulkinghorn the master of Lady
Dedlock's secret, implicates her as a suspect in his murder. But it
must also be recognized as the beginning of the chain of circumstances
that ends in his death, for it is the origin of his relation with Hortense
and of her grudge against him.

The movements of Esther's handkerchief are plotted with great
ingenuity, but there is more than ingenuity in the way these movements stitch mothers and children, living and dead, into a meaningful
pattern. After Esther has left the handkerchief over the body of Jenny's
dead baby, Lady Dedlock takes it up as a remembrance of the girl who,
she has now learned, is her daughter. In the scene where she reveals
their relationship to Esther, she carries it with her as an emblem of her
recognition. After her flight, Bucket finds it among her effects, sees
Esther's name on it, and realizes the truth of Lady Dedlock's position.
But he also realizes, when the time for the pursuit arrives, that Esther
will be a valuable ally if he has to persuade Lady Dedlock against suicide. In this way, the handkerchief is instrumental in bringing Esther
to her dead mother's side at the tragic moment when her parents are
united in death at the cemetery. The event is given extraordinary implications by the fact that up until the last moment Esther has mistaken Lady Dedlock for Jenny, another mother of another lost child,
with whom the shiftings of the handkerchief began.

The bundle of letters written by Lady Dedlock to her lover years
before the action of the novel makes a similar complex journey through
the labyrinths of the plot. When Bucket reveals that he has gained
possession of them, the reader is compelled to reconstruct this journey
and to recall that, after being kept in a secret place by Hawdon, the
letters came into Krook's hands at the death of his lodger and were
promised to Jobling and Guppy, who intended to transmit them to
Lady Dedlock. But Krook's death prevented this, and instead the
bundle made its way from the detritus of the cat's bed where Krook
kept it, and where Smallweed found it when he took over his dead
kinsman's effects, into the possession of Tulkinghorn, who learned

from it the meaning of Lady Dedlock's interest in the law-writer's handwriting. Ultimately, the letters were appropriated by Bucket when he searched the murdered man's office, and then demanded by Smallweed in a noisy scene with Sir Leicester. Guppy's warning that whatever secrets they contain are certain to be exposed convinces Lady Dedlock that she is about to be ruined, and leads directly to her flight. These trivial objects move through the novel like flotsam cast about in a violently churning medium; their movements mark the currents of the profound forces that pour through the novel, and of the inescapable relationships within it. The handkerchief forms an eloquent grouping of tragic mothers and children, and the letters, passing from forgotten obscurity into the grasp of merciless investigators, ultimately link the guilty lovers in a widely circling pattern of retribution.

The coincidences that are admittedly crucial to the plot of *Bleak House* have been defended on the grounds that they are exceptionally well concealed and that they serve to express moral doctrine; actually, such defenses only make them more objectionable. Dickens was not self-conscious about coincidences; he did not consider them faults, and introduced them freely, not because they were necessary to his plots, but for the sake of surprise. He also thought that accidental events could express positive truths. In justifying the death of Madame DeFarge in *A Tale of Two Cities,* he wrote: "Where the accident is inseparable from the passion and action of the character; where it is strictly consistent with the entire design, and arises out of some culminating proceeding on the part of the individual which the whole story has led up to, it seems to me to become, as it were, an act of divine justice." [4] But the feeling most relevant to the numerous coincidences of *Bleak House* is Dickens' belief that life itself is full of unexpected and arbitrary conjunctions. Every novel, after all, bases its action on certain pre-existing conditions. In *Bleak House,* such facts as Esther's parentage, Chancery's methods, Richard's weakness of character, and the location of the valid will are underlying truths of the scene that is being examined; they are not open to question and do not require demonstration, but are simply facts that await discovery. The major coincidences have a similar status, as premises peculiar to the life *Bleak House* surveys. They are established before the novel opens, and their effects on the action are presented with the same imaginative conviction, the same power to stimulate the suspension of disbelief, as the more plausible parts of the story. Dickens' narrative genius is

[4] Letter to John Forster [August, 1859], in *Nonesuch Letters,* III, 117.

usually strong enough to sustain them against the skepticism of a narrowly motivational view of life. When they are accepted within this context as meaningful instances, and not as mere lapses from conventional notions of realism, the coincidences of *Bleak House,* somewhat like those of Hardy's novels, are seen to embody a vital theme.[5]

Fully as important to the effect of *Bleak House* as the action itself is the symbolism, whose astonishing profundity and complexity have been described by J. Hillis Miller.[6] While the settings, characters, and events of Dickens' earlier novels sometimes rise to symbolic force, as Mr. Miller has shown, they ordinarily function as illustrations of the class of things to which they belong, rather than as true symbols. The workhouse in *Oliver Twist,* for example, is a condemnation of workhouses; Madeleine Bray in *Nicholas Nickleby* represents helpless womanhood forced into merciless marriage; and Mrs. Skewton in *Dombey and Son* stands for all vain women who refuse to acknowledge the effects of age. In spite of numerous foreshadowings of Dickens' later manner, in such figures as Fagin, Dombey, and Quilp, the earlier novels generally operate in this way. However, *Bleak House* exhibits a marked difference in emphasis. Its ostensible subject fails to correspond with the full weight of the novel's meaning, just as Aesop's animals fall short of participating in the moral conclusions of the fables. The subject achieves universality through a metaphoric leap; it becomes associated with generalities belonging to different categories from its own. Under the pressure of imaginative energy, it is forced into the symbolic transformation, whose power, as Carlyle observed, lies in its mystery.

Paradoxically, the symbolic potential of *Bleak House* seems to have originated in Dickens' strong feelings about the particulars which served as his symbols. There is no doubt that it was the injustices of Chancery, the horrors of poverty and London slums, the danger to health threatened by crowded cemeteries, and the follies of "telescopic philanthropy" as he encountered them in the England of his time that aroused his indignation. His passion about these things led him to dramatize and essentialize them into the static and readily understood exhibits that Mr. Garis identifies with the theatrical quality of his art. But it also led him to sense elusive implications in them and to resort

---

[5] For an excellent statement of this view, see W. J. Harvey's "Chance and Design in Bleak House," in *Dickens and the Twentieth Century,* eds. John Gross and Gabriel Pearson (London: Routledge & Kegan Paul Ltd., 1962), pp. 145–57.

[6] J. Hillis Miller, *Charles Dickens: The World of His Novels* (Cambridge, Mass.: Harvard University Press, 1958), pp. 160–224.

to the suggestive poetic symbolism described by Mr. Miller and other critics. The endless lawsuit which no one wants to continue and which no one can stop, whose immensity cannot be encompassed by any one mind, and which spreads random destruction among innocent victims is a criticism of the law, to be sure, but it is also an image of the impersonal "System" to which governments entrust their affairs, and further, as Mr. Miller puts it, becomes "a symbol in the novel of what it is to be in the world at all." Mr. Spilka is therefore undoubtedly right to see in it some of the metaphysical implications felt in Kafka's symbolism. The great Cause is a metaphor for the hopelessness of sorting out right from wrong in a world that lacks a living moral sense. Tom-all-Alone's is not merely an example of the need for slum clearance, not merely an apparatus for distilling the evils of society into concentrated form, but also a mysterious focus of retribution, "a secular inferno" [7] that punishes the innocent as well as the guilty in accordance with some covert and terrible system of justice.

The painted figure that points prophetically at the spot where the dead Tulkinghorn will lie after he has been murdered in his chambers is called Allegory. Dickens treats him with sarcasm, but often refers to him and to his indicative finger. *Bleak House* itself also constantly reverts to an allegoric mode through its major symbols. There are archetypal resonances in its treatment of Richard Carstone's obsession, Esther's parentage, Chesney Wold, the Court, and Tom-all-Alone's. Whenever these appear in the story they bring with them noticeable increments of feeling and significance, and establish relationships that transcend causality. They also condition its atmosphere, setting up what Tennyson, speaking of the *Idylls of the King*, called "a parabolic drift," and creating a fluid and reverberant medium within which every detail seems capable of a larger meaning. When Miss Flite first meets Esther and the cousins, she invites them to her room because "youth, and hope, and beauty are very seldom there." Her use of these abstractions seems perfectly innocent; but when we learn the names of her birds and see that their cage is a microcosm of the Court we realize that her remark predicts that the young people, too, will be trapped in Chancery. Old Turveydrop, Skimpole, and Vholes are not merely amusing minor characters, but also instances of the parasitism that infects society, like the institution of the law, whose first principle is to make

---

[7] This is Norman Friedman's excellent term for the scenes of poverty in *Bleak House*. See his article, "The Shadow and the Sun," *Boston University Studies in English*, III (1957), 147–66.

business for itself. This allegorical element functions as an alternative to coincidence, for, like coincidence, it expresses the sense that scattered people and events are somehow connected with each other and that, as Bucket puts it, all "are mixed up in the same business and no other."

Dickens' earlier novels, no matter how varied and digressive they may be, move in a single direction, along the line of the main action. But *Bleak House* creates quite a different effect. Many of the characters and events that appear at different points in the plot achieve a deeper significance when they are thought of as co-existing with each other within the context of the novel. The reader gathers their import through a process of lateral reference which generates parallels, contrasts, complements, and similar relationships, so that they become the elements of an integrated, complex, and inexhaustibly consequential design. Dickens seems to have been seeking new channels of relevance not found in traditional narrative methods, and the result, as Mr. Tindall suggests, is that there is something peculiarly modern about *Bleak House*, a speculation which is perhaps confirmed by the fact that many of the novel's inner relationships did not become apparent to readers until the twentieth century. Because its separate components gain much by being interpreted as comments on each other, and because the story is partly shaped by the narrative method, *Bleak House* has some traces of the self-sufficiency and self-reflexiveness that Roger Shattuck has identified as modes distinguishing modern from nineteenth-century art.[8] In the main, of course, it draws its subjects from actuality; but insofar as its experimental qualities broach unconventional narrative possibilities, its subject becomes the question of writing a novel, just as the subject of cubist and impressionist pictures may be said to be the question of making a picture. It seems to take a step or two, therefore, in the direction of the sort of modern art work whose real subject is itself. Also, when the relationships that crowd *Bleak House* are regarded as a design, the temporal elements associated with plot and story tend to be suppressed. The resulting effect approximates the simultaneity or spatialization that Joseph Frank has described as another distinctive characteristic of modern literature.[9]

[8] See *The Banquet Years* (Garden City, N.Y.: Doubleday & Company, Inc., 1961), pp. 327–28.
[9] See Joseph Frank, "Spatial Form in Modern Literature," in *The Widening Gyre* (New Brunswick, N.J.: Rutgers University Press, 1967), pp. 3–62.

Bleak House has many themes, but the dominant ones are perhaps those brought forward by the two main lines of the plot: justice and the meaning of the past. In his essay, Mr. Donovan points out that Dickens' way of treating justice resembles the one adopted by Plato in *The Republic*; Dickens' notion of justice also conforms to the definition offered by Socrates, that each shall have his own possessions and do his own work. The major statement made on this subject through the perverse processes of the Cause is echoed in the numerous instances of disproportion and inappropriateness that crowd the novel. Richard is perpetually unable to find his own work; Mrs. Jellyby directs her energies in the wrong directions; the young Mr. Turveydrop labors to support the idleness of his father; and Skimpole follows an ethical system that favors only himself. The fates of Hawdon and Jo raise crucial questions of social justice. It is not surprising that Mr. Jarndyce should have given up the hope of finding justice in the society described in the novel and should have retired to the refuge of Bleak House. The placid scene of Esther's married life at the conclusion is a similar refuge; it is an oddly irrelevant escape from the forces at work in the action of the story, not a victory over them.

But these forces are not invincible. At least two cases in the novel show that they can be defeated by those who have a firm vision of order and the courage to pursue it. Of all the characters, the one who struggles most successfully against circumstances to achieve not extravagant happiness but a destiny fit for her is Caddy Jellyby. Following instinctive urges, she makes a proper woman of herself with Esther's help, finds an adequate suitor, rebels against her contemptuous mother, takes in her neglected father, and embarks upon a prosaic marriage. At the end of the novel, the embittered and rebellious girl has become a conscientious and contented woman, though her life is a hard one. These are the materials of a realistic novel resembling George Moore's *Esther Waters*; in Caddy's story, Dickens did his work not by pitting his imagination against probability, as he often did, but by achieving a judicious distillation of it. Justice also emerges in the affairs of Rosa, who is enabled to go to her lover and escape the stain of scandal through Lady Dedlock's sacrifice. But there is another significant presence presiding over this rectification, that of Rouncewell, the ironmaster. The conception of justice associated with him and the class he represents prevails over that of Sir Leicester in the conflict that centers about Rosa; and it also prevails, morally, over the traditional order in which Sir Leicester has his place, but which is more specifically embodied in Chancery.

Tradition is a second leading theme in *Bleak House*. Like many Victorian novels, *Bleak House* can be viewed as the story of an effort to escape the moral impositions of a burdensome past, as a contest, to put it in its simplest terms, between the living and the dead. However, its criticism is directed not only against the past itself, but more specifically against the agencies society employs for interpreting it. The function of the Court is precisely that of determining how the fruits of the past shall be apportioned. The Court is seen as dangerous because, like Chesney Wold with its ghost, like Parliamentary government and the Dedlock family pride, it regards itself as an instrument for imposing the will of the dead upon the living. It is not surprising that the society it controls should be choked, like Krook's shop, with useless remnants of history.

But the most immediate treatment of the theme of the past is the story that begins with Lady Dedlock's sin and ends with Esther's happy marriage. The conflict between the commands of tradition and the needs of the present is foreshadowed in the scene where Esther's godmother interrupts her reading of the passage about the woman taken in adultery to quote instead St. Mark's call for vigilance against sin. Esther comes closest to accepting the traditional view about the sins of the past at the moment when she is walking near Chesney Wold, and fears that she has become the fulfillment of the prediction that the house of Dedlock would be betrayed when the steps of its ghost were heard on the terrace: ". . . my echoing footsteps brought it suddenly into my mind that there was a dreadful truth in the legend of the Ghost's Walk, that it was I who was to bring calamity upon the stately house; and that my warning footsteps were haunting it even then." However, she quickly rejects this interpretation of her story. Among those who seek to profit from bringing the past, in the form of Lady Dedlock's secret, back to life, are Smallweed, Hortense, and Tulkinghorn. On the other hand, Jarndyce's generosity is illustrated by his willingness to ignore Esther's irregular parentage. In asking her to marry him he rises above her "inheritance of shame," and in praising her to Woodcourt's mother he balances the "true legitimacy" of her virtuous character against the noble Welsh ancestry of which Mrs. Woodcourt ridiculously boasts.

Lady Dedlock's action in releasing Rosa comes close to being the decisive move in the struggle between tradition and the present; it is a blow against the pride of the aristocracy and sheds a stain on her husband's heritage, but it allows Rosa to find self-determination in accordance with the code of the new middle-class civilization. At the end of the novel, the contrast between the new Bleak House and Chesney Wold is the result of Lady Dedlock's decision and its sequels. Esther's home, which is held together by the affections and satisfactions of the present, not by archaic protocol, is a serene and idyllic little manor. But Chesney Wold has become a void of echoing passages where Sir Leicester listens absently as his sister reads to him through the long, dull evenings.

Like most Victorian novels written for publication as serials or in three-volume form, *Bleak House* is a compound novel with several interweaving plots and several distinct sets of characters. But it also has its own peculiar device for widening the range of the narrative, the two different points of view from which the story is alternately told. Dickens' narrators are his heroine, Esther, and an anonymous author-figure who is comparatively omniscient.[10] The general opinions of the two are similar; both sympathize with the poor and helpless, oppose burdensome traditions, and favor personal benevolence over abstract humanitarianism as a means of solving social problems. However, Dickens, no doubt in the interest of varying tone and avoiding repetitiveness, gave his narrators sharply differentiated styles and divided the material of his story between them. The arrangement was accepted without much question by his contemporaries. But modern readers, who feel that the angle from which a story is told may play a crucial part in determining its shape and meaning, cannot escape the sense that the split in Dickens' narrative method creates a corresponding fissure in the vision presented by the novel.

Having conceived of his main character as a modest, self-effacing girl who is painfully conscious of the unworthiness of her birth, yet capable of charity and generosity,[11] Dickens provides her with narrative material that is appropriate to her and serves to characterize her. Her interests do not go beyond personal and domestic matters; she is concerned with love affairs and family life, and with the pathos and sentiment these subjects generate. She expresses herself earnestly and sincerely but rarely comments on general questions and has no sense of

[10] The exact limits of this narrator's knowledge and his attitudes are defined in M. E. Grenander's "The Mystery and the Moral: Point of View in Dickens' *Bleak House,*" *Nineteenth Century Fiction,* X (1956), 301–5.

[11] According to the analysis of William Axton in "The Trouble with Esther," *Modern Language Quarterly,* XXVI (1965), 545–57.

large moral issues or social forces. The objective narrator is only a narrative voice, and not a fictional figure, but he displays nearly as much personal character as Esther does. He has a wide-ranging, energetic, and severely ironic sensibility. He is capable of vigorous satire about men and institutions, and of seeing such extensive fields as the law, the poor, and the nobility in a single panorama. When Esther confronts experiences with symbolic implications, such as Lady Dedlock's revelation or the ending of the Chancery suit, she can be profoundly moved, but is also baffled; the objective narrator, on the other hand, manipulates symbolic values intelligently and develops the death of Jo into a denunciation of the society he considers responsible for it. He is, above all, a sensitive and flexible observer; he conveys admirably the subtle undercurrents of Lady Dedlock's interviews with Tulkinghorn and Guppy, and can also treat the absurdities of political and aristocratic life with furious satire.

The contrasts between the two narrators are never made explicit, for each is limited to his own field of observation and shows no knowledge of the other. As a result, there are very few opportunities for comparing their reactions toward common experiences; but the few instances that do occur are significant. The limitations of Esther's mind appear when she naively describes Chesney Wold as picturesque and serene, in contrast to the objective narrator's depiction of "the place in Lincolnshire" as dreary and depressing. Their descriptions of Lady Dedlock are complementary rather than contradictory; this time it is Esther who knows more, for she comes to learn something about the cause of the frigid reserve which the other narrator can only describe. Particularly interesting are the differences of opinion about Guppy. Esther describes him as a confused and awkward fellow, as he no doubt appears to be in courting a girl who is his social superior. In the objective narrative, however, he is skillfully presented as an astute young legal aspirant handicapped by vulgarity of speech and manners who is nevertheless bold and tenacious.

The differences between the two narratives are not limited to matters of judgment. In style and subject they embody radically different modes of perception, which are not so much contradictory as foreign to each other. George Ford has shown the relevance to Dickens' novels of the two kinds of structure that Edwin Muir, in his *Structure of the Novel*, calls the novel of character and the dramatic novel.[12] Using a classifi-

---

[12] George Ford, *Dickens and His Readers* (Princeton, N.J.: Princeton University Press, 1955), p. 140.

cation strongly reminiscent of Lessing's contrast between instantaneous arts, like sculpture and painting, and arts of sequence, like music and literature, Muir distinguishes novels whose subject matter develops with the passing of time from those which seem to unfold in space. The first type focuses upon psychological or spiritual developments, while the second surveys the activities of fixed characters as they move from place to place. In *Bleak House* Dickens has intuitively formalized the distinction between these narrative principles by assigning one of them to each of his voices. In Esther's story, relationships change, the people undergo spiritual transformations, and the issues with which she is occupied ultimately find their resolutions. The world seen through her eyes resembles Muir's dramatic novel. But the objective narrator surveys a wide general scene inhabited by presences (both the "flat" characters and the unseen forces of social evil) which persist in unchanging form because they represent permanent situations or states of mind. The present tense of this narrative suggests that things do not change. At the end of the novel, the Court of Chancery continues, the destructive forces of Tom-all-Alone's are still at work, Chesney Wold endures. Even Lady Dedlock, Krook, and Tulkinghorn survive as figures of what Muir calls "almost mythical permanence."

These technical differences are not arbitrary, but appropriate to the moral views of the two narratives. "The values of the character novel," says Muir, "are social . . . the values of the dramatic novel individual or universal, as we choose to regard them . . . . These two types of the novel are neither opposites . . . nor in any important sense complements of each other; they are rather two distinct modes of seeing life; in Time, personally, and in Space, socially." [18] Accordingly, Dickens' objective narrator is concerned with evils that originate in social arrangements and arise from general forces that transcend any one life and operate independently of any one will. To him, Time is an irrelevance. In spite of the sensational events that occur, the social conditions he describes do not change significantly and the forces he observes are like enduring laws which render one period of time much like any other. But to Esther, Space does not matter. She is occupied with the minds and hearts of her domestic circle, and the rest of the world is meaningful to her only as a reflection of this narrow scene. In her dramatic narrative, moral values are matters of personal responsibility, and the people meet their destinies through the spiritual

[18] Edwin Muir, *Structure of the Novel* (New York: Harcourt, Brace & World, Inc., 1929), p. 63.

development or decline that can occur only with the passage of time.

According to Muir, the sacrifice of one dimension of actuality made by each of his narrative modes is the condition for achieving an effect of completeness and universality. We can readily see how this functions in the two narratives of *Bleak House*. It is, further, striking that the completeness in each case amounts to a very different thing. The two recitals are not complementary to each other, like those in *Lord Jim*, nor destined for containment within one framework, like those in *The Ring and the Book*. Instead, they exhibit the mutual irrelevance that characterizes Muir's narrative modes. As Joseph I. Fradin has said, ". . . there is no specious bridging of the gap, no attempt to impose a false wholeness of view. The debate between the two voices carries, without the genuine possibility of resolution, beyond the conclusion, and the limitations of the story they tell." [14] The two narratives defy *any* attempt to formulate their relationship; they do not confirm, augment, balance, or directly contradict each other. They are simply different from each other. Thus, it appears that the disparities of the double narrative strongly qualify the cohesive effect created by the plot and symbolism; the latter work to trace relationships among separate elements, but the former opens unexpected divisions in issues that seem unified and simple.

The divided point of view is only the most general example of a principle so fully present in the narrative technique of *Bleak House* that it overrides both Dickens' expressed indignation and the optimism of the ending to take its place as the novel's ultimate verdict upon the reality it surveys. One night, as Esther is going to the brickmaker's cottage, the contrast between the cold light of the lingering sunset and the "lurid glare" that hangs over London leads her to sense that there is a similar duality about herself, that she is not really the person she is supposed to be. The incident illustrates the problem of identity posed by the contrasts and reduplications that pervade the novel. The effect of significant difference in similarity, or ironic similarity within difference, is struck time and again in such pairings as Chesney Wold and Bleak House, the world of fashion and the Court, the Court and Krook's shop. Through a process of doubling often noted by the critics, nearly every character in the novel becomes a member of a pair or a series of figures that varies or contrasts one essential characteristic. Esther, the orphan and homeless child, is paralleled by Charley, and the contagion that involves them with Jo emphasizes the kinship of all

[14] In "Will and Society in *Bleak House*," *PMLA*, LXXXI (March, 1966), 95–109.

three. Lady Dedlock, by disguising herself as Hortense at one time and exchanging clothes with Jenny at another, sets up copies of herself. There are two Wills, two Bleak Houses, and even Mrs. Bayham Badger has had three husbands. Dickens seems to have been possessed by a restless indecision that led him to embody each of his ideas in various forms, and to rehearse every question in a different key or with a second cast of characters.

This impulse is reflected also in some odd redundancies of action. Esther is blinded and scarred by her disease; but these effects disappear. The discovery of the truth about her birth would have served as the ideal motivation for Tulkinghorn to increase his pressure on Lady Dedlock; but Dickens brings this about instead by resorting to Lady Dedlock's concern for Rosa. A marriage between Esther and Jarndyce would have been a possible dénouement; but the whole action of their courtship and engagement is made into a puzzling irrelevancy by her marriage to Woodcourt. It is easy to see why none of these circumstances is allowed to exert a meaningful influence on the story. To make Esther the cause of her mother's ruin and death, or to exact from her the sacrifices of blindness or marriage to Jarndyce as demonstrations of her selflessness—these logical conclusions were too austere for a story meant to demonstrate the beneficent control of Providence. They are therefore relegated to the status of shadow episodes, so that the edifying effects of their moralism can be exploited while less painful resolutions are worked out through other means.

The doubling of characters and narrators, like the shadow episodes, is a part of Dickens' effort to gain a more complete view of the issues than a single attack could establish. He had not yet reached the point where he could probe moral questions through the sustained development of situation and character. Not until *Great Expectations*, which was written eight years later, did he succeed in plaiting strands of good and evil together into conflicts of genuine moral complexity. In *Bleak House* we find that virtue and vice are distinct from each other, spread through the world in clearly marked separate packets. Nevertheless, Dickens achieves complexity through counterpart characters, whose individual moral status is unambiguous but who are linked in such a way that innocence is related to guilt, power to helplessness, benevolence to selfishness. In this art of counterparts, however, the differences count as heavily as the similarities; the parallels move together but also pull against each other. If their resemblances show that responsibility and suffering are shared by all, their diversities create a relative effect and discourage final judgment. Esther sees the world as a single moral spectacle; but *Bleak House* as a whole presents it as an inconclusive, kaleidoscopic multiverse of shifting perspectives that eludes clear definition. The relevance of one part of it to another remains problematic. Krook's way of writing one letter at a time so that he can never see a whole word at once is not only Dickens' lesson about the nature of reality, it is also his method.

The profound and subtle oscillation introduced by the alternating narrative voices prevents *Bleak House* from formulating its moral problems in fixed images. They appear in ambiguous form, as matters of social responsibility when seen through the eyes of the objective narrator, and as matters of private conscience when seen through Esther's. When Jo, after seeing Lady Dedlock disguised as Hortense, and mistaking Hortense for her, meets Esther, who also resembles her, he whispers incredulously, "Is there *three* of 'em then?" This experience is perhaps the quintessential one in the world portrayed by *Bleak House*. It is a realm of nightmare correspondences, where things both are and are not themselves, where there is always something strange about the familiar and something familiar about the strange. Its moral dilemmas can never be fully localized or resolved, for they are always accompanied by past shadows or present counterparts that are out of control; instead, they continually return to haunt the conscience in new yet oddly repetitive forms, like the terrible regenerations of the great Cause itself.

PART ONE

Interpretations

The Anatomy of Society

by Edgar Johnson

Cumulatively, [the] characters make *Bleak House* both an anatomy of society and a fable in which its major influences and institutions are portrayed by means of sharply individualized figures. They are instruments through which the meaning of the story is enlarged and extended to one of the broadest social significance. But everywhere its statements are conveyed not in abstractions but embodied in character and action organically related to the analysis. Archibald MacLeish is wrong in saying that a poem should not mean but be: like any work of literature, it may legitimately both mean and be. Into the very existence of *Bleak House* Dickens has precipitated the understanding of nineteenth-century society that he has achieved.

His method is at the same time realistic and figurative. Mrs. Jellyby, never seeing anything nearer than Africa, Mrs. Pardiggle, forcing her children to contribute their allowances to the Tockahoopo Indians, are themselves; but they are also the types of a philanthropy that will do nothing to diminish the profitable exploitation of England's poor. Mrs. Pardiggle will hand out patronizing little booklets to debased brickmakers who are unable to read; she will not work to obtain them a living wage or decent homes with sanitary facilities. Neither she nor Mrs. Jellyby will do a thing to abolish a pestilent slum like Tom-all-Alone's or to help an orphan vagrant like Jo.

"He is not one of Mrs. Pardiggle's Tockahoopo Indians," Dickens says bitterly;

he is not one of Mrs. Jellyby's lambs, being wholly unconnected with Borrioboola-Gha; he is not softened by distance and unfamiliarity; he is

"The Anatomy of Society." From Charles Dickens: His Tragedy and Triumph *by Edgar Johnson (New York: Simon and Schuster, Inc., 1952), II, 769–79. Copyright © 1952 by Edgar Johnson. Reprinted by permission of Little, Brown and Company.*

not a genuine foreign-grown savage; he is the ordinary home-made article. Dirty, ugly, disagreeable to all the senses, in body a common creature of the common streets, only in soul a heathen. Homely filth begrimes him, homely parasites devour him, homely sores are in him, homely rags are on him: native ignorance, the growth of English soil and climate, sinks his immortal nature lower than the beasts that perish. Stand forth, Jo, in uncompromising colours! From the sole of thy foot to the crown of thy head, there is nothing interesting about thee.[1]

Even more marked, however, in *Bleak House* is the use of poetic imagery and symbolism to underline and parallel the meaning of its patterns. The fog of the opening chapter is both literal and allegorical. It is the sooty London fog, but it covers all England, and it is the fog of obstructive procedures and outmoded institutions and selfish interests and obscured thinking as well. Miss Flite's caged birds symbolize the victims of Chancery, and the very names she has given them in her insanity are significant: "Hope, Joy, Youth, Peace, Rest, Life, Dust, Ashes, Waste, Want, Ruin, Despair, Madness, Death, Cunning, Folly, Words, Wigs, Rags, Sheepskin, Plunder, Precedent, Jargon, Gammon, and Spinach." "That's the whole collection," adds Krook, the sham Lord Chancellor, "all cooped up together, by my noble and learned brother." [2] Later, Miss Flite adds two more birds to the collection, calling them "the Wards in Jarndyce." [3] And always outside the cage lurks the cat Lady Jane, waiting, like the lawyers, to seize and tear any that might get free. Lady Jane is sometimes seen as a tiger and sometimes as the wolf that cannot be kept from prowling at the door. Mr. Vholes, skinning his tight black gloves off his hands as if he were flaying a victim, is constantly described, as are the other lawyers, in metaphors drawn from beasts of prey. And there is a further imagery of spiders spinning their traps, entangling flies within strand upon strand of sticky and imprisoning filaments, hanging their meshes everywhere in gray and dusty clotted webs.

The most elaborately worked out of these symbols is the parallel between Krook and the Lord Chancellor. "You see I have so many things here," Krook explains,

of so many kinds, and all, as the neighbours think (but *they* know nothing), wasting away and going to rack and ruin, that that's why they have given me and my place a christening. And I have so many old parch-

---

[1] *Bleak House*, Chapter XLVII.
[2] *Ibid.*, Chapter XIV.
[3] *Ibid.*, Chapter LX.

mentses and papers in my stock. And I have a liking for rust and must and cobwebs. And all's fish that comes to my net. And I can't abear to part with anything I once lay hold of (or so my neighbours think, but what do *they* know?) or to alter anything, or to have any sweeping, nor scouring, nor cleaning, nor repairing going on about me. That's the way I've got the ill name of Chancery. *I* don't mind. I go to see my noble and learned brother pretty well every day when he sits in the Inn. He don't notice me, but I notice him. There's no great odds betwixt us. We both grub on in a muddle.[4]

And to sharpen the point still more, as Lady Jane, at his bidding, rips a bundle of rags with tigerish claws, he adds, "I deal in cat-skins among other general matters, and hers was offered me. It's a very fine skin, as you may see, but I didn't have it stripped off! *That* warn't like Chancery practice though, says you!"[5]

Nor are these sharp and bitter strictures unjustified by the actualities. The Day case, nowhere near settled at the time Dickens wrote, dated from 1834, had always involved seventeen lawyers and sometimes thirty or forty, and had already incurred costs of £70,000.[6] The case of Gridley, the man from Shropshire, was based upon an actual case that had been called to Dickens's attention.[7] Jarndyce and Jarndyce was suggested by the notorious Jennings case, involving the disputed property of an old miser of Acton who had died intestate in 1798, leaving almost £1,500,000. When one of the claimants died *in 1915* the case was still unsettled and the costs amounted to £250,000.[8]

Such facts give cogency to Dickens's conclusions:

The one great principle of the English law is, to make business for itself. There is no other principle distinctly, certainly, and consistently maintained through all its narrow turnings. Viewed by this light it becomes a coherent scheme, and not the monstrous maze the laity are apt to think it. Let them but once perceive that its grand principle is to make business for itself at their expense, and surely they will cease to grumble.

"But not perceiving this quite plainly," the laity *do* grumble, and then the

---

[4] *Ibid.*, Chapter V.
[5] *Ibid.*, Chapter V.
[6] *Ibid.*, preface. Vol. II, p. 481, *Letters of Charles Dickens, The Nonesuch Dickens*, Nonesuch Press, London, 1938.
[7] *Ibid.*, preface.
[8] *Ibid.*, preface. *Dickensian*, XI, 2.

respectability of Mr. Vholes is brought into powerful play against them. "Repeal this statute, my good sir?" says Mr. Kenge to a smarting client, "repeal it, my dear sir? Never, with my consent. Alter this law, sir, and what will be the effect of your rash proceeding on a class of practitioners very worthily represented, allow me to say to you, by the opposite attorney in the case, Mr. Vholes? Sir, that class of practitioners would be swept from the face of the earth. Now you cannot afford—I will say, the social system cannot afford—to lose an order of men like Mr. Vholes. Diligent, persevering, steady, acute in business. My dear sir, I understand your present feelings against the existing state of things, which I grant to be a little hard in your case; but I can never raise my voice for the demolition of a class of men like Mr. Vholes." [9]

The respectability of Mr. Vholes "has even been cited with crushing effect before Parliamentary committees" and been no less reiterated in private conversations affirming

that these changes are death to people like Vholes: a man of undoubted respectability, with a father in the Vale of Taunton, and three daughters at home. Take a few steps more in this direction, say they, and what is to become of Vholes's father? Is he to perish? And of Vholes's daughters? Are they to be shirtmakers, or governesses? As though, Mr. Vholes and his relations being minor cannibal chiefs, and it being proposed to abolish cannibalism, indignant champions were to put the case thus: Make man-eating unlawful, and you starve the Vholeses! [10]

But the law is only the archetype of those vested interests that plunder society under the guise of being society, that strangle the general welfare, that grow fat on the miseries of the poor. It is one of the instruments that give "monied might the means abundantly of wearying out the right," [11] the visible symbol behind which lurk the forces of greed and privilege spinning their labyrinthine webs of corruption. Spread out over the fair English landscape are Chesney Wold, with its noble dignity, its green garden terraces and stately drawing rooms, Bleak House, with its orderly comfort and generous master, Rouncewell's, with its productive and self-respecting industry. But Rouncewell's is no more than part of the whole—a part, too, that will reveal its own dark evils under the deeper analysis of *Hard Times*. Bleak House, at its best and for all its warm intentions, is itself helplessly enmeshed and can make only frustrated gestures to reach out a help-

---

[9] *Bleak House,* Chapter XXXIX.
[10] *Ibid.,* Chapter XXXIX.
[11] *Ibid.,* Chapter I.

ing hand. And Chesney Wold has its corollary and consequence in Tom-all-Alone's and the wretched hovels of the brickmakers: its dignity is built on their degradation.

Chesney Wold and Tom-all-Alone's are thus also symbols in the symbolic structure. For Dickens does not mean that Sir Leicester Dedlock, or even the aristocracy as a class, is personally responsible for social evil, any more than are the Lord Chancellor or Carboy and Kenge or Inspector Bucket. Individually they may all be amiable enough, but they are instruments of a system in which the stately mansion and the rotting slum represent the opposite extremes. Inspector Bucket, officially the bloodhound of the law, is personally a bluff and kindhearted fellow, Conversation Kenge merely a florid rhetorician, the Lord Chancellor a harmless old gentleman. And to Sir Leicester, who epitomizes the system, Dickens is chivalrously magnanimous.

Sir Leicester is a good feudal landlord, a kind and generous master to his servants, loyal to his family, devoted to his wife. "He is a gentleman of strict conscience, disdainful of all littleness and meanness, and ready, on the shortest notice, to die any death you may please to mention rather than give occasion for the least impeachment of his integrity. He is an honourable, obstinate, truthful, high-spirited, intensely prejudiced, perfectly unreasonable man." [12] Beneath his high demeanor and occasional absurdity there is a core of true nobility. When he learns the story of Lady Dedlock's past, and falls moaning to the floor, paralyzed and unable to speak, his devotion to his wife and his distress at her flight are greater than the horror of the revelation, and his faltering hand traces upon a slate the words, "Full forgiveness. Find——" [13]

But, for all his private virtues, he has no hesitation about trying to bully or buy a victory in Parliamentary elections, although he bitterly resents the corrupt opposition to his own purposes that makes this expensive course necessary. The "hundreds of thousands of pounds" required to bring about the triumph of his own party he blames on the "implacable description" of the opposition and the "bad spirit" of the people. His dependent spinster cousin, the fair Volumnia, with her rouge, her still girlish ways, and her little scream, is innocently unable to imagine the need for this enormous outlay; Sir Leicester freezes her with his displeasure: "It is disgraceful to the electors. But as you, though inadvertently, and without intending so unreasonable

[12] *Ibid.*, Chapter II.
[13] *Ibid.*, Chapter LVI.

a question, asked me 'what for?' let me reply to you. For necessary expenses." [14]

The "implacable" opposition is, of course, merely a rival faction contending for the spoils of office, and no matter which party wins, the country is still dominated by wealth and privilege manipulating all the puppetry of political juntas. This is true even when the candidates of Mr. Rouncewell the ironmaster capture a few seats, and will continue to be true when they fill the House, despite Sir Leicester's gasping conviction that "the floodgates of society are burst open, and the waters have—a—obliterated the landmarks of the framework of the cohesion by which things are held together!" [15] All that the rising power of the industrialists really means is that they too will force their way into the coalition of exploitation formed by their predecessors, the landed aristocracy, the lawyers and politicians, the merchants, and the bankers.

The political aspects of this situation Dickens conveys with a wonderful burlesque brilliance. "His description of our party system, with its Coodle, Doodle, Foodle, etc.," writes Bernard Shaw, "has never been surpassed for accuracy and for penetration of superficial pretence." But Shaw's feeling that Dickens "had not dug down to the bedrock of the imposture" is derived from a failure to notice that Dickens portrayed Tom-all-Alone's and the brickmakers as much more than a mere indictment of "individual delinquencies, local plague-spots, negligent authorities." [16] In reality Dickens links all these phenomena with each other, the political bargains and combinations no less so than the slow-moving chicaneries of law.

Lord Boodle points out to Sir Leicester that the formation of a new Ministry lies

> between Lord Coodle and Sir Thomas Doodle—supposing it to be impossible for the Duke of Foodle to act with Goodle, which may be assumed to be the case in consequence of the breach arising out of that affair with Hoodle. Then, giving the Home Department and the Leadership of the House of Commons to Joodle, the Exchequer to Koodle, the Colonies to Loodle, and the Foreign Office to Moodle, what are you to do with Noodle? You can't offer him the Presidency of the Council; that is reserved for Poodle. You can't put him in the Woods and Forests; that is hardly good enough for Quoodle. What follows? That the country is

[14] *Ibid.,* Chapter XI.
[15] *Ibid.,* Chapter XI.
[16] Shaw, Preface to *Great Expectations.*

shipwrecked, lost, and gone to pieces . . . because you can't provide for
Noodle!

On the other hand, the Right Honourable William Buffy, M.P., con-
tends across the table with some one else, that the shipwreck of the
country—about which there is no doubt; it is only the manner of it that
is in question—is attributable to Cuffy. If you had done with Cuffy what
you ought to have done when he first came into Parliament, and had
prevented him from going over to Duffy, you would have got him into
alliance with Fuffy, you would have had with you the weight attaching
as a smart debater to Guffy, and you would have brought to bear upon
the elections the wealth of Huffy, you would have got in for three coun-
ties Juffy, Kuffy, and Luffy, and you would have strengthened your ad-
ministration by the official knowledge and business habits of Muffy. All
this, instead of being as you now are, dependent upon the mere caprice
of Puffy! [17]

Beyond their witty parody of the language of political manipulation, these two paragraphs ingeniously exploit the mere ludicrous
rhyming sounds of their alphabetical succession of names and the de-
rogatory implications of many of those names. Boodle is not an au-
spicious name for a politician, nor do Noodle and Poodle convey the
most promising insinuations. Doodle and Noodle were names of two
of the characters in one of the versions of Fielding's burlesque *Tom
Thumb*. And from the time immediately before his reporting days
Dickens may well have remembered that the notoriously incompetent
Lord Dudley, Secretary of State for Foreign Affairs under the Duke of
Wellington in 1828, was widely known as Lord Doodle,[18] and that
"doodle" meant to trifle or to make droning noises. Guffy, Huffy,
Muffy, and Puffy may also be made to yield derisive associations, and
possibly even Buffy, Cuffy, and Luffy.

With biting satire Dickens paints the ensuing political corruption.

England has been in a dreadful state for some weeks. Lord Coodle would
go out, Sir Thomas Doodle wouldn't come in, and there being nobody
in Great Britain (to speak of) except Coodle and Doodle, there has been
no Government. . . . At last Sir Thomas Doodle has not only con-
descended to come in, but has done it handsomely, bringing in with him
all his nephews, all his male cousins, and all his brothers-in-law. So there
is hope for the old ship yet.

[17] *Bleak House*, Chapter XII.
[18] London *Times* Lit. Sup., July 28, 1950, p. 476, "John Wilson Croker as Gossip,
I," by Alan Lang Strout, quoting a letter of Croker's to Lord Hertford, January 8,
1828.

In the process, he "has found that he must throw himself upon the country—chiefly in the form of sovereigns and beer," "in an auriferous and malty shower" while "mysterious men with no names" rush backward and forward across the country on secret errands. Meanwhile Britannia is "occupied in pocketing Doodle in the form of sovereigns and swallowing Doodle in the form of beer, and in swearing herself black in the face that she does neither." [19]

All this structure of venality rises upon a foundation of exploitation, destitution, and misery. We are shown the wretched hovels of the brickmakers at St. Alban's, "with pigsties close to the broken windows," old tubs "put to catch the droppings of rainwater from a roof, or . . . banked up with mud into a little pond like a large dirt-pie." [20] Within their damp and musty rooms we see their dwellers, "a woman with a black eye nursing a poor little gasping baby by the fire; a man all stained with clay and mud, and looking very dissipated, lying at full length on the ground, smoking a pipe; a powerful young man, fastening a collar on a dog; and a bold girl, doing some kind of washing in very dirty water." [21] As Professor Cazamian points out, contemporary official reports all more than justify the hideous picture.[22]

Into this scene Mrs. Pardiggle pushes her way, hectoring its inhabitants in her loud, authoritative voice and ignoring the growling resentment of the man on the floor.

"I wants a end of these liberties took with my place. I wants a end of being drawed like a badger. . . . Is my daughter a-washin? Yes, she *is* a-washin. Look at the water. Smell it! That's wot we drinks. How do you like it, and what do you think of gin, instead! Ain't my place dirty? Yes, it is dirty—it's nat'rally dirty, and it's nat'rally onwholesome; and we've had five dirty and onwholesome children, as is all dead infants, and so much the better for them, and for us besides. Have I read the little book wot you left? No, I ain't read the little book wot you left. There ain't nobody here as knows how to read it; and if there wos, it wouldn't be suitable to me. It's a book fit for a babby, and I'm not a babby. If you was to leave me a doll, I shouldn't nuss it. How have I been conducting of myself? Why, I've been drunk for three days, and I'd a been drunk four, if I'd a had the money. Don't I never mean for to go to church? No, I don't never mean for to go to church. I shouldn't be expected there, if

[19] *Bleak House,* Chapter XI. Could Doodle's nephews, cousins, and brothers-in-law have suggested Sir Joseph Porter's "sisters and his cousins and his aunts," in Gilbert's *Pinafore*?
[20] *Ibid.,* Chapter VIII.
[21] *Ibid.,* Chapter VIII.
[22] Louis Cazamian, *Le roman social en Angleterre* (1830–1850), Paris, 1904, p. 297.

I did; the beadle's too gen-teel for me. And how did my wife get that black eye? Why, I giv' it her; and if she says I didn't, she's a Lie!" [23]

Worse still is the urban slum of Tom-all-Alone's, a black, dilapidated street of crazy houses tumbling down and reeking with foul stains and loathsome smells, dripping with dirty rain, and sheltering within its ruined walls a human vermin that crawls and coils itself to sleep in maggot numbers on the rotting boards of its floors among fetid rags. "Twice, lately, there has been a crash and a cloud of dust, like the springing of a mine, in Tom-all-Alone's; and each time a house has fallen. These accidents have made a paragraph in the newspapers, and have filled a bed or two in the nearest hospital. The gaps remain, and there are not unpopular lodgings among the rubbish." [24] There dwells Jo, with his body exuding a stench so horrible that Lady Dedlock cannot bear to have him come close to her; and thence comes Jo, munching his bit of dirty bread, and admiring the structure that houses the Society for the Propagation of the Gospel in Foreign Parts. "He has no idea, poor wretch, of the spiritual destitution of a coral reef in the Pacific, or what it costs to look up the precious souls among the cocoa-nuts and bread-fruit." [25] And when Jo lies dead of neglect, malnutrition, and disease, the narrative swells into an organ-toned and accusing dirge: "Dead, your Majesty. Dead, my lords and gentlemen. Dead, Right Reverends and Wrong Reverends of every order. Dead, men and women, born with Heavenly compassion in your hearts. And dying thus around us every day." [26]

Counterpointed with the death of Jo is that of Richard Carstone, for high-spirited and generous youth, with every advantage, is no less prey to the infection of an acquisitive society than helpless ignorance and misery. All Richard's buoyancy and courage, his gentleness and frankness, his quick and brilliant abilities, are not enough to save him. Gradually he becomes entangled in the fatal hope of getting something for nothing, stakes everything on the favorable outcome of the Chancery suit, neglects his capacities, fosters his careless shortcomings, dissipates the little money he has, feverishly drifts into suspicion and distrust of his honorable guardian, argues that Mr. Jarndyce's appearance of disinterestedness may be a blind to further his own advantage in the case. How, Richard asks, can he settle down to anything? "If

[23] *Bleak House,* Chapter VIII.
[24] *Ibid.,* Chapter XVI.
[25] *Ibid.,* Chapter XVI.
[26] *Ibid.,* Chapter XLVII.

you were living in an unfinished house, liable to have the roof put on or taken off—to be from top to bottom pulled down or built up—tomorrow, next day, next week, next month, next year,—you would find it hard to rest or settle." [27] By early manhood his expression is already so worn by weariness and anxiety that his look is "like ungrown despair." [28] Not until it is too late, and he is dying, does he speak of "beginning the world," and confess his mistakes and blindnesses to his wife. Esther Summerson reports his words:

> "I have done you many wrongs, my own. I have fallen like a poor stray shadow on your way, I have married you to poverty and trouble, I have scattered your means to the winds. You will forgive me all this, Ada, before I begin the world?"
>
> A smile irradiated his face, as she bent to kiss him. He slowly laid his face down upon her bosom, drew his arms closer round her neck, and with one parting sob began the world. Not this world, O not this! The world that sets this right.
>
> When all was still, at a late hour, poor crazed Miss Flite came weeping to me, and told me she had given her birds their liberty.[29]

Richard Carstone and poor Jo, Miss Flite driven insane, Gridley dying broken on the floor of George's shooting gallery and George in the toils of the moneylenders, Mr. Tulkinghorn shot through the heart in his Lincoln's Inn Fields chambers beneath the pointing finger of allegory, Sir Leicester humbled, heartbroken, and paralyzed, Lady Dedlock dead, disgraced, and mud-stained outside the slimy walls of the pauper graveyard where her lover lies buried—all are swept on to frustration or defeat in the titanic intensity of this dark storm of story. Everywhere the honest, the generous, the helpless, the simple, and the loving are thwarted and crippled. John Jarndyce, the violently good master of Bleak House, can rescue only a distressingly small number of those he sets out to save. In a life of poverty and struggle imposed by a society where nature itself is deformed and tainted, poor Caddy Jellyby and her husband Prince Turveydrop can give birth only to an enfeebled deaf-and-dumb child. For *Bleak House* (like Shaw's *Heartbreak House,* of which it is a somber forerunner) is in its very core symbolic: *Bleak House* is modern England, it is the world of an acquisitive society, a monetary culture, and its heavy gloom is implied by the very adjective that is a part of its title.

[27] *Ibid.,* Chapter XXXVII.
[28] *Ibid.,* Chapter XLV.
[29] *Ibid.,* Chapter LXV.

Structure and Idea in *Bleak House*

by *Robert A. Donovan*

Edmund Wilson called *Bleak House* a novel of the "social group"; E. K. Brown called it a "crowded" novel. Both statements are undeniable; neither one offers any particular help in understanding how Dickens brought artistic order to a novel as broad in scope as *Bleak House*. A number of astute critics have grappled with the problem of structure in this novel, and the general tendency of their labors, at least in recent years, has been to refer the problem, not to such an obvious structural principle as plot, but to the infinitely more complex and subtle principle of language. Thus Norman Friedman, J. Hillis Miller, and Louis Crompton all seek the novel's fullest and deepest statement of meaning in the patterns of diction, imagery, and symbolism.[1] The insights derived from this species of criticism may be valuable; all three of these critics have important contributions to make. But so narrow a critical perspective has its dangers as well as its attractions. The art of the novel, as Dickens conceived and practiced it, was still a story-telling art, and though it is certainly true that his language, at least in the mature works is richly charged and implicative, I do not believe that any acceptable reading of *Bleak House* can be reached without reference to those ingredients which are constituted by its participation in a story-telling tradition—I mean specifically, plot and the closely related layers of character and point of view.

First the plot. "Plot" here means the record of events, organized according to some intelligible principle of selection and arrangement. The narration of unrelated (even though sequential) events does not

---

"*Structure and Idea in* Bleak House" *by Robert A. Donovan. From ELH, XXIX, No. 2 (1962), 186–201. Copyright © 1962 by The Johns Hopkins Press. Reprinted by permission of The Johns Hopkins Press.*

[1] Norman Friedman, "The Shadow and the Sun: Notes Toward a Reading of *Bleak House*," *Boston University Studies in English, III* (1957), 147–66; J. Hillis Miller, *op. cit.*; Louis Crompton, "Satire and Symbolism in *Bleak House*," *Nineteenth-Century Fiction,* XII (1957–58), 284–303.

give rise to plot; time sequence alone does not organize experience in
any meaningful way. The loosest kind of organization is supplied by
character; events may be related in that they happen to the same
person, whether or not they reveal any growth, either in the character
himself, or in our understanding of him. A somewhat more complicated structure arises when events are related to each other by their
common illustration of a single idea or of several related ideas. Finally,
events may be organized according to a causal sequence in which
each successive event is in some way caused by the one which precedes
it. Now only in the last sense does plot function as the unifying element in a story, for though it is possible for a story to *have* a plot in
either of the first two senses, we would, in those cases, probably refer
the story's unity to, respectively, character or theme.

It is virtually impossible to subsume the events of *Bleak House* into
a single causal sequence, or even into several, as long as we understand
by "events" what that word normally signifies, that is, births, deaths,
betrothals, marriages, whatever, in short, is likely to be entered in the
family Bible, and perhaps also such other occurrences (of a less public
and ceremonial nature) as quarreling, making love, eating, drinking,
working, etc., which may have an interest of their own. *Bleak House* is
full enough of "events" in this sense; I count nine deaths, four marriages, and four births. The difficulty is in assigning their causes or
their consequences. What are we to make of the death of Krook for
example? The question is not one of physiology; I don't propose to
reopen the question of spontaneous combustion. The question is properly one of psychology: how is Krook's death related to the play of
human motives and purposes? The answer, of course, is that it is not
so related at all; it is a simple *deus ex machina* whose only artistic
justification is to be sought at the level of symbolism. Rick Carstone's
death, by contrast, is integrated with plot, for though its physiological
causes may be as obscure as those of Krook's death, its psychological
causes are palpable and satisfying. Or take Esther's marriage to Allan
Woodcourt. Is it, like the marriage of Jane Austen's heroines, the inevitable culmination of a pattern of events, or is it merely a concession
to popular sentiment, like the second ending of *Great Expectations*?
A great many, perhaps most, of the "events" of *Bleak House* consist of
such hard and stubborn facts—stubborn in that they are not amenable
to the construction of any intelligible law; they exist virtually un-
caused, and they beget effects which are quite disproportionate to their
own nature or importance. Events have a way of taking us by surprise,

for even though Dickens is careful to create an appropriate atmosphere whenever he is about to take someone off, the time and manner of death are generally unpredictable.

The artistic center of the novel is generally taken to be Chancery, but if so it seems to me that Chancery functions as a symbol, not as a device of plot. We are permitted glimpses from time to time of what "happens" in Chancery, but Jarndyce and Jarndyce obviously follows no intelligible law of development, and so it is meaningless to talk about a Chancery plot or subplot. Furthermore, though Chancery affects the lives of many, perhaps all, of the characters in *Bleak House*, it does not do so in the sense that significant events take place there. The only event in the Court of Chancery that proves to have significant consequences for the people outside is the cessation of Jarndyce and Jarndyce when the whole property in dispute has been consumed in legal costs. But this is itself a conclusion reached by the stern requirements of economics rather than by the arcane logic of the law. Chancery affects men's lives the way God does, not by direct intervention in human affairs, but by commanding belief or disbelief.

In a few instances events align themselves in something approaching a genuine causal sequence. The story of Rick Carstone, for example, who undergoes a slow moral deterioration because he is gradually seduced into believing in Chancery, provides an example of a meaningful pattern of events. But Rick's story is neither central, nor altogether satisfying, principally, I believe, because it is observed only at intervals, and from without.[2] It remains true that it is all but impossible to describe what happens in *Bleak House* by constructing a causal sequence of events.

The difficulty largely disappears, however, when we stop trying to discover a more or less systematic pattern of events, and try instead to define the organization of the book in terms of discovery, the Aristotelian anagnorisis. The plot, in this case, is still woven of "events," but the word now signifies some determinate stage in the growth of awareness of truths which are in existence, potentially knowable, before the novel opens. Events, in the original sense of that term, become important chiefly as the instrumentalities of discovery. Krook's death, for example, leads to the unearthing of an important document in Jarndyce and Jarndyce, and incidentally to the disclosure

---

[2] As Edgar Johnson has argued, Dickens was not to do justice to this theme until *Great Expectations* (*Charles Dickens: His Tragedy and Triumph* [New York, 1952], p. 767).

of a complex web of relations involving the Smallweed, Snagsby, and Chadband families. The murder of Tulkinghorn or the arrest of Trooper George are red herrings, designed to confuse the issue, but ultimately they make possible the complete unveiling of the pattern of human relations that it is the chief business of the novel to disclose. The progressive discovery of that pattern is, then, the "plot" of the novel, and it constitutes a causal sequence, not in that each discovery brings about the next, but in that each discovery presupposes the one before. We need to know that Lady Dedlock harbors a secret which she regards as shameful before we can discover the existence of some former connection between her and Nemo, and we need to be aware of that connection before we can add to it the more important discovery that Esther is the daughter of Nemo and Lady Dedlock. And so on, until the whole complicated web stands clearly revealed.

This kind of structure is, as everyone knows, the typical pattern of the detective story. Such fundamentally human concerns as crime and punishment lie outside the scope of detective fiction, in which the murder may take place before the story begins, and the retribution may finally catch up with the murderer after it ends. The plot of the detective story consists simply in the discovery—withheld, of course, as long as possible—of the one hypothesis which will account for all the disparate facts or "events" that make up the story. The interest is centered, in classical specimens of the genre, not in the events, but in the process by which the events are rendered meaningful, ordinarily in the activity of the detective as he proceeds toward a solution. *Bleak House,* of course, has many detectives. Not counting the unforgettable Inspector Bucket "of the Detective," a great many characters are at work throughout the novel at unravelling some private and vexing problem of their own: Mr. Tulkinghorn, stalking Lady Dedlock's secret with fearful persistency, or Mr. Guppy approaching the same mystery from Esther's side, or Mrs. Snagsby endeavoring to surprise her husband's guilty connections, or even Esther herself, troubled by the riddle of her own mysterious origin and still more mysterious participation in the guilt of her unknown mother. But the presence or activity of a detective is incidental to the main scheme of such fiction, from *Oedipus the King* onward, to present a mystery and then solve it. The beginning, middle, and end of such an action can be described only in terms of the reader's awareness; the beginning consists of the exposition in which the reader is made aware of the mystery, that is of the facts that require explanation; the end consists of his reaching a full understanding of the mystery which confronted him, for when all is known the story must come to an end. The middle, then, is comprised of his successive states of partial or incorrect knowledge.

The mystery presents itself, in the typical detective novel, with crystalline purity. Someone has been murdered; the problem is to discover, in the graphic but ungrammatical language of the usual cognomen, Who done it? In *Bleak House* the problem is somewhat different. It is true that there is a murder, and that the murderer must subsequently be picked out of three likely suspects, but the main mystery, the one that sustains the motion of the whole book and gives it a unity of plot, is not a question of determining the agent of some past action (though the mystery *may* be formulated in these terms) so much as it is a question of establishing the identity of all the characters involved, and in the world of *Bleak House* one's identity is defined according to his relations to other people. Two recent writers, James H. Broderick and John E. Grant, consider that the novel is given its shape by Esther's successful quest for identity, or place, in the society of the book,[3] and I see no reason why the establishment of identity, not merely for Esther, but for all or most of the characters may not provide a workable principle of structure. Esther's identity is secure when she discovers who her parents are, and this is certainly the heart of *Bleak House*'s mystery, but that discovery comes shortly after the middle of the book, when Lady Dedlock discloses herself to Esther. The novel is not complete until all the relations of its various characters are recognized and established (or re-established) on some stable footing. Sir Leicester Dedlock must adjust his whole view of the world to conform to the discovery he makes about his wife; harmony must be restored between Mr. Jarndyce and Rick; Esther must discover her true relation to Mr. Jarndyce—and to Allan Woodcourt. Even the minor characters must be accounted for: Trooper George must become once again the son of Sir Leicester's housekeeper and the brother of the ironmaster; Mr. and Mrs. Snagsby must be reconciled as man and wife; all misunderstandings, in short, must be cleared away.

One of the most curious features of *Bleak House,* one of the attributes which is most likely to obtrude itself and bring down the charge of staginess is Dickens's careful husbandry of characters. That he disposes of so many may perhaps be worthy of remark, but still more remarkable is the fact that he makes them all, even the most obscure, serve

[3] "The Identity of Esther Summerson," *Modern Philology*, LV (1958), 252–58.

double and triple functions. Mr. Boythorn, for example, the friend
of Mr. Jarndyce who is always at law with his next-door neighbor, Sir
Leicester Dedlock, doubles as the rejected suitor of Miss Barbary,
Esther's aunt. And it is surely a curious coincidence which sends Rick,
when he is in need of a fencing teacher, to Trooper George, who is
not only related to the Chesney Wold household through his mother,
but also deeply in debt to Grandfather Smallweed (Krook's brother-
in-law), and of course he has served under Captain Hawdon, Esther's
father. Mrs. Rachael, Miss Barbary's servant, turns up again as the
wife of the oily Mr. Chadband, and even Jenny, the brickmaker's wife,
appears fortuitously to change clothes with Lady Dedlock. These examples, which might easily be multiplied, irresistibly create the impression, not of a vast, chaotic, utterly disorganized world, but of a
small, tightly ordered one. That the novel thus smacks of theatrical
artifice constitutes a threat to the "bleakness" of *Bleak House,* for we
are never confronted, in this world, by the blank and featureless faces
of total strangers, the heart-rending indifference of the nameless mob;
all the evils of this world are the work of men whose names and
domestic habits we know, and for that reason, it would appear, are
deprived of most of their terrors.

Perhaps the most serious charge that can be brought against the
artistry of *Bleak House* grows out of some of the characteristic features
which I have been discussing. How can the discerning reader avoid
being offended, it will be argued, by a novel which obviously wants to
say something serious and important about society, but at the same
time contrives to say it in the most elaborately artificial way possible?
How can we be serious about social criticisms which come to us through
the medium of the most sensational literary genre, and are obscured
by every artifice of melodrama? The objection seems to be a damaging
one, but I wonder if Dickens's employment of the techniques of the
detective story and of melodrama may not enforce, rather than
weaken, his rhetorical strategy. The plot, as I conceive it, consists of
the progressive and relentless revelation of an intricate web of relations
uniting all the characters of the novel, by ties of blood or feeling or
contract. And Dickens's assignment of multiple functions to the minor
characters is merely a means of reinforcing and underscoring our sense
that human beings are bound to each other in countless, often unpredictable ways. It is difficult to see how Dickens could have found a
clearer, more emphatic way of drawing up his indictment against society for its failure to exercise responsibility than by his elaborate
demonstration of human brotherhood.

The bleakness of *Bleak House* is the sense of hopelessness inspired by the knowledge that men and women, subjected to the common shocks of mortality, will nevertheless consistently repudiate the claims which other people have on them. The sense of hopelessness is intensified and made ironic by the closeness, figuratively speaking, of their relations to other people (sometimes, of course, the closeness is literal, as in the hermetic little community of Cook's Court, Cursitor Street). It is appropriate that the novel should be shaped by discoveries rather than by events, for the sense of hopelessness, or bleakness, can hardly be sustained in a world that can be shaped to human ends by human will. The events of this novel are accidental in a double sense; most of them are unplanned and unpredictable, and they are moreover nonessential to the view of human experience that Dickens is concerned to present. Human relations, the ones that are important, are not constituted by events (though they may be revealed by events—Esther's smallpox, for example), because events just *happen,* they follow no intelligible law either of God or man. Human relations are inherent in the nature of society, and the duty of man is therefore not something arbitrary and intrinsically meaningless which can be prescribed and handed down to him by some external authority (like law); it is discoverable in, and inferrable from, his social condition and only needs to be seen to command allegiance. The tragedy of *Bleak House* is that awareness of human responsibility invariably comes too late for it to be of any use. Nemo's or Coavinses', or Jo's membership in the human race is discovered only after his death, and Sir Leicester Dedlock awakens to recognition of the true nature of the marriage bond only when his wife has gone forth to die. Still, it is important to *have* that awareness, and the most effective way to produce it, surely, is to make its slow growth the animating principle of the novel.

If we choose to talk about the plot of *Bleak House* as constituted by a growing awareness of human relations and human responsibilities, sooner or later we must raise the question: *Whose* awareness? The problem of point of view is so important in the detective story, in fact, that it is most often met by the creation of a special point-of-view character. The classical instance, of course, is Dr. Watson, but Dr. Watson has had countless avatars. *Bleak House* is enough of a detective story so that it must reckon with some, at least, of the problems that Dr. Watson was invented to solve. The mystery must be preserved, so the narrator's perspicacity must have rather clearly defined limits, but at the same time the mystery must take hold of the reader, so the narrator must possess lively human sympathies and be capable of moral insights which are as just and true as his practical judgments are absurd. Such considerations impose limits on the choice of a narrative perspective for *Bleak House,* but there are other considerations which affect that choice too. The mystery whose solution dominates the novel is not such a simple, or at any rate such a limited problem as identifying a particular character as the criminal; Dickens's villain is a whole society, and its guilt cannot be disclosed by a sudden dramatic unveiling. Furthermore Dickens is only partly concerned with the disclosure of the truth to the reader; a more fundamental matter is the discovery by the participants of the drama themselves of the relations in which they stand toward all the other members of society. It is the story of Oedipus on a large scale.

Because of the staggering breadth of Dickens's design the selection of a narrative point of view is extraordinarily difficult. If he chooses an omniscient, third person point of view a good deal of the emotional charge is lost, particularly if the narrator remains (as he must) sufficiently aloof from the actions and events he describes to avoid premature disclosures. On the other hand, a first person narrator suffers equally important disabilities. The most immediately obtrusive of these is physical and practical. How can a single character be expected to participate directly in all the relations the novel is about? How can one character contribute evidence (as opposed to hearsay) of events which take place in London, in Lincolnshire, and in Hertfordshire, sometimes simultaneously? The difficulty could be partly met by the selection of one of those numerous characters like Tulkinghorn or Mr. Guppy or young Bart Smallweed who seem to be always on the "inside," in control of events simply because they know about them, yet one difficulty yields only to be replaced by another. Characters like Tulkinghorn obviously lack the "lively human sympathies" which give to the first person point of view its special value, and as narrator Tulkinghorn (who is in any case disqualified on the more fundamental ground that he is killed) would offer no advantage over the omniscient point of view. The obvious solution to this dilemma is to have both points of view, alternating the narration between them.

The dual point of view in *Bleak House* has always served as a speck of grit, around which the commentators have secreted their critical pearls. E. M. Forster regards it as a blemish, though he thinks Dickens's talent can make us forget it: "Logically, *Bleak House* is all to pieces, but Dickens bounces us, so that we do not mind the shiftings of the

view point." [4] Others defend the double point of view as artistically
appropriate.[5] I regard the device as a concession to a necessity that I
can see no other way of circumventing, but there are perhaps one or
two things to be said about it.

Bleak House is a novel without a center. There is no single character
to whom the events of the story happen, or with reference to whom
those events are significant. It is not even possible (as I have already
argued) to understand the novel as a unified system of co-ordinate plots
or of plot and sub-plots. Except for this want of a center the novel
might be compared to a spider web in which each intersection represents a character, connected by almost invisible but nonetheless tenacious filaments to a circle of characters immediately surrounding him,
and ultimately, of course, to all the other characters. But the spider
web has a center (and a villain), so a more appropriate comparison
might be made to a continuous section of netting, or better still, to
the system of galaxies which make up the universe. It appears to a
terrestrial observer that all the other galaxies are receding from him at
an unthinkable rate of speed, implying that his own post of observation constitutes the center of things. Yet the centrality of his own
position is merely a function of his special point of view. So with *Bleak
House.* Esther is, in this special sense, the "center" of the novel, not
because she so regards herself, but because she supplies the central
observation point, because relations are measured according to their
nearness or farness from her just as astronomical distances are measured in parsecs—heliocentric parallax (in seconds of arc) as recorded
for a terrestrial observer. To pass, for example, from Esther to Nemo
(or some other intermediate character) to George to Matthew Bagnet
is to move, so to speak, from the center outward. But Esther is not
really the center of the novel. To think of her as such is to destroy
or at least to do serious violence to Dickens's view of the world, and
transform his indictment of society into a sentimental fable. To deprive
the novel of its specious center, to provide it with a new perspective
which, like stereoscopic vision, adds depth, is an important function
of the omniscient point of view.

Dickens's handling of that portion of the narrative which is related
by the omniscient observer (roughly half of the novel) is, on the
whole, masterly. I do not know that any critic denies the full measure

---

[4] *Aspects of the Novel* (London, 1927), p. 108.
[5] For example, M. E. Grenander, "The Mystery and the Moral: Point of View in
Dickens's 'Bleak House,'" *Nineteenth-Century Fiction*, X (1955–56), 301–305.

of praise for things like the opening paragraph or two of the novel, that magnificent evocation of the London fog which has been quoted so often that I may be excused from doing so here. The laconic, unemotional style, with its sentence fragments and present participles in place of finite verbs, the roving eye, which, like the movie camera mounted on an overhead crane, can follow the action at will, are brilliantly conceived and deftly executed. It is a descriptive style emancipated from the limitations of time and space, and accordingly well-suited to its special role in the novel. But Dickens's control of this narrator is uneven. Superbly fitted for the descriptive passages of the novel, his tight-lipped manner must give way to something else in passages of narration or, still more conspicuously, in those purple rhetorical passages that Dickens loves to indulge in. As a narrator, the omniscient persona (now speaking in finite verbs in the present tense) suffers somewhat from a hollow portentousness, a lack of flexibility, and a rather pointless reticence which can become annoying, as in the narration of Tulkinghorn's death (though here again the descriptive powers get full play). The requirements of consistency do not seem to trouble Dickens when it is time to step forward and point the finger at the object of his satire. The narrative persona is dropped completely when Dickens speaks of Buffy and company, or apostrophizes the "right" and "wrong" reverends whom he holds responsible for the death of Jo. But these passages win us by their obvious sincerity, and we need not trouble ourselves over the fact that the mask has been inadvertently dropped. To insist on a rigorous consistency here is to quibble over trifles, for generally speaking the third person narration is adroit and effective.

The focus of discontent with the manipulation of point of view in *Bleak House* is Esther Summerson. Fred W. Boege writes:

> There is nothing necessarily wrong with the idea of alternating between the first and third persons. The fault lies rather with Dickens' choice of a medium for the first-person passages. David Copperfield demonstrates that the conventional Victorian hero is not a commanding figure in the center of a novel. Esther Summerson proves that the conventional heroine is worse; for the hero is hardly more than colorless, whereas she has positive bad qualities, such as the simpering affectation of innocence.[6]

I think it is essential to distinguish carefully between Esther's qualities as "heroine" and Esther's qualities as narrator, for though the two

[6] "Point of View in Dickens," *PMLA,* LXV (1950), 94.

functions are not wholly separate, it ought to be possible to have a bad heroine who is a good narrator and vice versa. As a heroine she clearly belongs to a tradition that we tend to regard as hopelessly sentimental and out of date. She is sweet-tempered and affectionate, and she is also capable and strong and self-denying. The first two qualities almost invariably (at least within the conventions of Victorian fiction) render their possessor both unsympathetic and unreal. One thinks of Amelia Sedley or Dinah Morris or Dickens's own Agnes Wickfield, and prefers, usually, the society of such demireps as Becky Sharp or Lizzie Eustace. Still, Esther's strength of character ought to save her, and give her a genuine hold on our regard, except for the fact that as narrator she is faced with the necessity of talking about herself, and her modest disclaimers ring false. When she tells us that she is neither good, nor clever, nor beautiful she forfeits a good deal of the regard that her genuinely attractive and admirable qualities demand. Esther the heroine is in a sense betrayed by Esther the narrator into assuming a posture that cannot be honestly maintained.

Whatever one thinks of Esther as a person, the important question at the moment is her discharge of the narrator's responsibility. The sensibility which is revealed by her attributes as a character (the term "heroine" is somewhat misleading) is of course the same one which will determine the quality of her perceptions and insights as narrator, and it is here, I think, that some confusion arises, for it is generally assumed that Esther's simplicity, her want of what might be called "diffractive" vision, the power of subjecting every experience to the play of different lights and colors, is held to undermine or even destroy her value as narrator. We have become so used to accepting the Jamesian canons of art and experience that we refuse validity to any others. The attitude is unfortunate, not to say parochial. For James "experience" (the only kind of experience that concerned the artist) was constituted by the perception of it. "Experience," he writes in "The Art of Fiction,"

is never limited, and it is never complete; it is an immense sensibility, a kind of huge spider web of the finest silken threads suspended in the chamber of consciousness, and catching every air-borne particle in its tissue. It is the very atmosphere of the mind; and when the mind is imaginative . . . it takes to itself the faintest hints of life, it converts the very pulses of the air into revelations.

This conception of experience is at the root of James's conception of the art of the novel, for it prescribes that the simplest kind of happening may be converted to the stuff of art by a sufficiently vibrant and sensitive point of view character. To a Lambert Strether the relations of Chad Newsome and Mme. de Vionnet are subtle, complex, and beautiful, because he is; but to another observer the same liaison is common and vulgar. Strether possesses what I have chosen to call diffractive vision, the ability to see a whole spectrum where the vulgar can see only the light of common day.

How can poor little Esther Summerson manage to perform the same function as a character with the depth and resonance of Lambert Strether? The answer, obviously, is that she can't. But I must hasten to add that she doesn't have to. The ontological basis of James's fiction is radically different from that of Dickens's; for in James what seems is more important than what is, and he accordingly requires a perceiving intelligence of the highest order. In Dickens, on the other hand, though he too is concerned with the characters' awareness, the relations which they are to perceive have a "real" existence which is not contingent on their being seen in a certain way. For this reason Esther does not have to serve as the instrument of diffraction; the light is colored at its source. To the sensitive Jamesian observer a single human relation appears in almost an infinite number of lights, and a single act may be interpreted in many ways. But Dickens does not work that way, at least not in *Bleak House*. Here the richness and infinite variety of human experience are suggested by the sheer weight of example, by the incredible multiplication of instances, and the narrator's chief function is simply to record them.

When Socrates and his friends Glaucon and Adeimantus differed over the nature of justice and injustice, Socrates proposed to settle the dispute, in the passage of the *Republic* from which my first epigraph is taken, by constructing an imaginary and ideal state in order to see how justice originates. The method is not at all unlike that of Dickens, who proposes to investigate the abstraction "injustice" by seeing how it arises in an imaginary replica of the real world. Both methods assume that what is universal and abstract is rendered most readily intelligible by what is particular and concrete, and furthermore that the particular and concrete establish a firmer hold on our feelings than the universal and abstract. For both Plato and Dickens are concerned not only with making justice and injustice understood, but with making them loved and hated, respectively. The method is perhaps suggestive of allegory, but it differs in important ways from any technique of symbolic representation. It is a species of definition which proceeds by attempting to specify the complete denotation of the thing to be defined. To the question, "What is Justice?" Plato replies by showing us his republic, perfect in all its details, and saying, "Justice is here." To a similar question about injustice Dickens need only reply by unfolding the world of *Bleak House.*

Let me particularize briefly. One of the important ethical abstractions the novel deals with is charity (a useful check list of such abstractions might be derived from the names of Miss Flite's birds). Dickens nowhere provides a statement of the meaning of this concept except by supplying a wide range of instances from which the concept may be inferred. Mrs. Jellyby (for example), Mrs. Pardiggle, Mr. Quale, and Mr. Chadband demonstrate various specious modes of the principal Christian virtue, and Captain Hawdon, Mr. Snagsby, Mr. Jarndyce, and Esther provide glimpses of the genuine article. None of these characters, and none of the acts by which they reveal their nature can be said to *stand for* the general idea, charity; collectively they *are* charity, which is thus defined by representing, on as ample a scale as possible, its denotation. Similarly with the whole spectrum of moral ideas and human relations in *Bleak House;* Dickens offers his main commentary, not by names or labels, certainly not by analysis, and not even by symbolic analogues (though he uses them). His principal technique is the multiplication of instances. To say that in a novel which is as richly and palpably symbolic as *Bleak House* symbolism is unimportant would be in the nature of an extravagant paradox, and I have no intention of going so far. I wish only to direct attention toward a narrative method which seems to me to have been strangely neglected by comparison with the symbolism which has proved so fruitful of insight.

At any rate, I think Esther is vindicated as narrator. The narrative design of the novel really requires only two qualities of her, both of which she exemplifies perfectly. In the first place, she should be as transparent as glass. The complex sensibility which is a characteristic feature of the Jamesian observer would be in Esther not simply no advantage, it would interfere with the plain and limpid narration she is charged with. We must never be allowed to feel that the impressions of characters and events which we derive from her are significantly colored by her own personality, that the light from them (to revert to my optical figure) is diffracted by anything in her so as to distort the image she projects. One partial exception to this generalization implies the second of the two characteristics I have imputed to her. In the second place, then, we require of Esther sufficient integrity, in a literal sense, to draw together the manifold observations she sets down. The most complex and elaborate act of synthesis is reserved for the reader, but to Esther falls the important choric function of suggesting the lines along which that synthesis should take place by drawing her observations together under a simple, traditional, and predictable system of moral values. If Esther occasionally strikes us as a little goody-goody, we must recall her function to provide a sane and wholesome standard of morality in a topsy-turvy world.

No critic, surely, can remain unimpressed by the richness of *Bleak House,* a quality which is both admirable in itself and characteristically Dickensian. But the quality which raises the novel to a class by itself among Dickens's works is its integrity, a product of the perfect harmony of structure and idea. Edmund Wilson long ago saluted *Bleak House* as inaugurating a unique genre, "the detective story which is also a social fable," but he provided no real insight into the method by which these radically unlike forms were made to coalesce. The secret, I believe, is partly in that instinctive and unfathomable resourcefulness of the artist, which enables him to convert his liabilities into assets, to make, for example, out of such an unpromising figure as Esther Summerson, just the right point of view character for the first-person portion of the novel. But the real greatness of *Bleak House* lies in the happy accident of Dickens's hitting upon a form (the mystery story) and a system of symbols (Chancery) which could hold, for once, the richness of the Dickensian matter without allowing characters and incidents to distract the reader from the total design. The mysterious and sensational elements of the plot are not superimposed on the social fable; they are part of its substance. The slow but relentless disclosure of the web of human relations makes a superb mystery, but what makes it a monumental artistic achievement is that it is also and simultaneously one of the most powerful indictments of a heartless and irresponsible society ever written. *Bleak House* is the greatest of Dickens's novels because it represents the most fertile, as well as the most perfectly annealed, union of subject and technique he was ever to achieve.

Style and Unity in *Bleak House*

by *Leonard W. Deen*

With the multiplied characters of Charles Dickens' *Bleak House* (1853) the expansibility of the Victorian novel comes close to its limit. The novel is roughly halfway over before Dickens has introduced the last of his proliferating cast of characters. Some of the minor characters exist at a great distance from the parent trunk; the branches have branches, and these in turn have *their* branches. Dickens is hard put to it to involve all his *dramatis personae* in some kind of plot; and the elaborate climaxes are often attended by people who *are* got on stage, even if they are only meddling. In its apparent attempt to sum up a whole society—peerage, lawyers, industrialists, shopkeepers, preachers, philanthropists, brickmakers, and crossing sweepers—*Bleak House* runs the risk of becoming a disorganized aggregation rather than a unified work of art.

The disorder of this vast system seems to be increased by its division into spheres of experience which are, or at first sight appear to be, almost completely unrelated. The two major worlds are the one experienced by Esther Summerson, and the panoramic one unfolded by the "anonymous" author. The major peculiarity of *Bleak House* is that the story is narrated by two distinct voices, only one of which belongs to a character in the novel. The anonymous speaker is not, properly speaking, "omniscient"; he doesn't *know* everything, and he does not have the key to anyone's consciousness, but he does *see* everything, and his eye is extraordinarily far-ranging. To take the two points of view at their most extreme difference, Esther's story is a melodramatic personal narrative, the author's an "external" descriptive narrative in which the greatest distinction of tone is to be found in the ironic descriptive pieces which manage the shift from one

"Style and Unity in Bleak House*" by Leonard W. Deen. From* Criticism, *III, No. 3 (Summer, 1961), 206–18. Copyright © 1961 by the Wayne State University Press. Reprinted by permission of the Wayne State University Press and the author.*

setting to another. The split into two very different points of view, each with its dominant tone, very much complicates the already complex plot and full universe of *Bleak House*. In spite of these difficulties, the novel does not disintegrate. To demonstrate the kind of unity it does possess is perhaps the best way of getting at its peculiar values.

Esther's story is primarily about parents and children and their impoverished relationships. Her narrative begins with her "escape" from a cruel aunt-stepmother and her absorption into the fairy-tale simplicity and security of Bleak House, where John Jarndyce has established a cozy inviolable retreat, and surrounded himself by children. The burden of Esther's story, whether it concerns Bleak House or London, is the perversion or crippling of the family and the child. Caddy Jellyby is ignored by her mother, who is more interested in philanthropy; the Pardiggle children are made monsters by a "philanthropic" mother's extortion of charity from them; Turveydrop is a parasite on his son. Harold Skimpole is an adult whose peculiar hypocrisy is to pretend that he is an entirely free, charming, and irresponsible child; and as child, of course, he can only ignore his duties as husband and father. Richard Carstone, when he dies, leaves his wife with a yet unborn child. "Charley" Neckett is orphaned, with a family of brothers and sisters to care for; Jo has neither parents nor relatives. Confronted by this astonishing array of the abandoned and the misbegotten, Esther spends her life trying to establish surrogate families. To people of her own age—Richard, Ada Clare, Charley, and Caddy—she plays mother. With Jarndyce she plays at housekeeping, and she is at the same time his "daughter" and his fiancée.

The submerged motive in Esther's life which becomes increasingly definite is her search for a mother. When her mother turns out to be Lady Dedlock, we see that the "mystery" of Esther's parentage is charged with as much social as personal significance. Esther is related in ways she does not understand with social worlds whose existence she is scarcely aware of. The split source of the narrative in *Bleak House* is a function of this larger mystery. It allows Dickens to create groups which are apparently (but only apparently) unconnected; and the convergence of the two narrative lines reveals the interconnectedness of the "separate" worlds and characters of the novel. The necessary relationships of blood, of feeling and responsibility, irresistibly assert themselves. The melodrama and the mystery turn on the fact that the fashionable world of the Dedlocks, Chancery Lane, and the hell of Tom-all-Alone's are all inescapably related. Mystery is ironically transformed into moral criticism.

Esther's narrative, though its final unity is of subject or theme, has a personal and emotional center of reference. It thus has some of the unifying advantages of plot, of referring events to dominant characters. The unity of the "author's" part of the novel, on the other hand, depends almost entirely on the fusion of theme and dominant tone. The anonymous narrative centers on the discrepancy between reality and appearance—between surface and depth, pretension and fact, anachronism and progress, dead ritual and live act. The tone is marked by an energetic irony suppressing an enormous violence of feeling. Style and attitude are Carlylean. An elaborate system of ironic imagery exposes the falsity or emptiness of the conventional social symbols— many of which pass for human beings.

The style establishes itself with immense authority in the first chapter. A panoramic movement centers London in Chancery, and reduces both to a single complex image of mud and fog: the fog hinting at universal obfuscation; the mud suggesting the prehistoric world of the flood, still unevolved, while it "accounts for" the ritual futility, the slipping and sliding, of the lawyers' activity. All London is reduced to a single pattern. The lawyers in Chancery mime the people outside; they are "mistily" engaged, "tripping one another up on slippery precedents, groping knee-deep in technicalities." From Mr. Tangle, honorifically addressing the Lord High Chancellor, "slides" out a word very like *mud:* "Mlud." "Thus, in the midst of the mud and at the heart of the fog, sits the Lord High Chancellor in his High Court of Chancery," like the extinct megalosaurus that Dickens mentioned earlier, except that the Chancellor is unaccountably not extinct. Chesney Wold, the ancestral seat of the Dedlocks, is in the first, definitive description also the world of the flood; and the deluge motif, twice announced, continues to reappear, with variations. In Chapter XIX (to take a single example) the flood has temporarily receded: "The Temple, Chancery Lane, Serjeants' Inn, and Lincoln's Inn even unto the Fields, are like tidal harbours at low water; where stranded proceedings, offices at anchor, idle clerks lounging on lopsided stools that will not recover their perpendicular until the current of Term sets in, lie high and dry upon the ooze of the long vacation."

In the anonymous narrative particularly, characters are used metonymically: they exist less for their own sake than for their ability to characterize their "world" or their class. Volumnia Dedlock (a "peachy cheeked" and "skeleton throated" "charmer," no longer young) perfectly images the "perpetual stoppage" the Dedlocks oppose to the "moving age" in which they live. Similarly, individuals (in an exaggeration of Dickens' usual mode of characterization) may be represented by parts of their persons. The family grandiosity of the Dedlocks takes up its residence in Sir Leicester's ears. When the ironmaster Rouncewell assaults them with what Sir Leicester considers "Wat Tylerism" he is astounded, but he is "obliged to believe a pair of ears that have been handed down to him by such a family."

One of the dominant ironic images exposing the discrepancy between fact and pretension and linking widely separated characters in the novel is that of empty containers, or surfaces which have no depth. The extremely righteous Chadband is not only a smoking oil factory, but a vessel, and not so much a vessel of the spirit of God as a "gorging vessel," always requiring to be filled. The same glossing over of the inane or the non-existent is managed by whole families and social orders, and by officially constituted authority. The Dedlocks of the past are represented entirely by their tombs and portraits, as the living fashionable world is represented by its mirrors, and Lady Dedlock by her particularly handsome and imposing portrait. Tulkinghorn's funeral is attended not by his upper-class clients, but by "inconsolable carriages": "The peerage contributes more four-wheeled affliction than has ever been seen in that neighbourhood. . . . The Duke of Foodle sends a splendid pile of dust and ashes, with silver wheel-boxes, patent axles, all the last improvements, and three bereaved worms, six feet high, holding on behind, in a bunch of woe." . . . Krook, reduced to a small heap of ashes by his spontaneous combustion, is nevertheless buried in a six-foot coffin, the court having insisted that "the fiction of a full-sized coffin should be preserved, though there is so little to put in it." And the desk which Vholes repeatedly strikes for Richard Carstone's benefit, staunchly averring, " 'This desk is your rock sir!' " sounds "as hollow as a coffin."

The thematic and tonal integrity of the anonymous narrative is achieved largely by exploiting the unifying possibilities of internal analogy and parody. Settings, characters, and motifs mock one another, as in distorting mirrors. The result is an elaborate system of interlocking worlds.

As I have already suggested, the linkage is often by dominant images, which give to varied settings a common and pervasive tonality. But the effect is never simple or static. One controlling image follows, without superseding, another. Chancery, at first all mud and fog, is later reflected in Krook's rag and bottle shop; and the rust, must, and cobwebs to which Krook is so devoted introduce new images for Chancery, which are developed later (in Chapter XIX, for example): "Over all the legal neighbourhood, there hangs, like some great veil of rust, or gigantic cobweb, the idleness and pensiveness of the long vacation." Both Tulkinghorn and Vholes, lawyers and animals of prey, have a particular liking for dust. Tulkinghorn's offices are a "lowering magazine of dust." Vholes' desk, when he strikes it, sounds as if "ashes were falling on ashes, and dust on dust." Krook's shop is later summed up by its heaps of worthless paper, an image exploited particularly in the Smallweeds' ratlike investigations of Krook's mountains of paper after they inherit his belongings. Finally, the development returns full circle in the closing chapters. When the Jarndyce suit in Chancery is brought to a close because the costs of the trial have exhausted the estate, the whole suit is finally reduced to a single image: the tons of paper recording the endless processes of the trial which are dumped in the courtroom.

Sometimes the connection between distinct settings is established by their allusion to a common myth. The suggestion in the first chapter that Chancery is hell (in the phrase "the outermost circle of such evil") is much more strongly asserted in the description of Krook's shop. Krook's roomer, Nemo, is said to have sold himself to the devil (who is both Krook and Lord High Chancellor), and Krook is on fire within —a smouldering which is to culminate in his being violently consumed by his own evil in the spontaneous combustion episode. The Smallweed establishment, where Grandfather Smallweed is several times scorched by being placed too near the fire, and where he occupies his idle time by watching the "fire —and the boiling and the roasting," is also a foretaste of hell, and Trooper George is in no doubt as to Grandfather Smallweed's eternal fate. The third version of hell is Tom-all-Alone's. When Inspector Bucket and Mr. Snagsby, heroic visitors, descend into the underworld the crowd is "like a concourse of imprisoned demons," "flitting, and whistling, and skulking about them."

Bleak House is full of persons whose main function is parody, who repeat the serious or the pathetic in the comic, the realistic or the melodramatic in the surrealistic or bizarre. Little Swills is a deliberate and habitual mimic who by parodying a "scene of real life"—the inquest into Nemo's death—turns it into a kind of folk ballad. Guppy, a minnow in the sharky sea of lawyers, unconsciously parodies Inspector Bucket. Before Bucket has even begun his investigations, Guppy in his own blunderingly cunning way has gone far towards solving the mystery of Esther's birth. In the sentimentality, disloyalty, and egregious confidence of his "love" for Esther, Guppy is a kind of parody-foil to Allan Woodcourt. Mrs. Snagsby's violently impotent jealousy ("busily laying trains of gunpowder" in her imagination) parodies the more dangerous and melodramatic jealousy of the murderous Mlle. Hortense. And Krook is of course a monstrous parody of the Lord High Chancellor.

The same systematic use of analogy and parody that organizes the "author's" narrative links the two narratives and helps to make of them a complex whole. Turveydrop, for example, in Esther's narrative, crosses its boundaries to become an absurd parody of the passé dandyism of the fashionable world of the author's narrative:

> He was a fat old gentleman with a false complexion, false teeth, false whiskers, and a wig. He had a fur collar, and he had a padded breast to his coat, which only wanted a star or a broad blue ribbon to be complete. He was pinched in, and swelled out, and got up, and strapped down, as much as he could possibly bear. . . . he stood poised on one leg, in a high-shouldered, round-elbowed state of elegance not to be surpassed. He had a cane, he had an eye-glass, he had a snuffbox, he had rings, he had wristbands, he had everything but any touch of nature. . . . (XIV)

Finally, the motifs of Esther's story are sometimes reflected in the other narrative. Bleak House is a fairy-tale world of orphans and fairy "godfather" where people habitually communicate in tag-ends of nursery rhymes. Esther herself is a kind of Cinderella who busies herself about the household, and whose devotion to Jarndyce is rewarded by his transformation into Allan Woodcourt, the inhabitant of a new and cozier Bleak House. The Smallweed family, as described by the anonymous voice, is an ironic negation of the childish world and the fairy-tale motif of Esther's story. No Smallweed, for generations, has ever been young, except Grandmother Smallweed, who in the utter decline of her faculties is enjoying her first childhood. Skimpole, in Esther's story, has, on the other hand, never grown up. Everywhere in the novel, youth and age trade places. Tulkinghorn has "aged without experience of genial youth," and Judy Smallweed "never owned a doll, never heard of Cinderella, never played at any game.

. . . And her twin brother couldn't wind up a top for his life. He knows no more of Jack the Giant Killer, or of Sinbad the Sailor, than he knows of the people in the stars" (XXI). The four Smallweeds are "ghastly cherubim"; Grandmother Smallweed is a "broomstick witch," and Grandfather is not only a "goblin" and "harlequin" but a "doll" and "puppet." As horrible dolls and globins, the nightmares of childish fantasy, the Smallweeds are perverse distortions of Esther's experience and of the Bleak House world.

Mystery, treated melodramatically in Esther's story, is often treated comically or satirically by the "author"—as in Guppy's and Weevle's spying on Krook, only to be frightened out of their wits by his macabre and inexplicable combustion. And the pastoral profusion of Boythorn's house in the country, where Esther convalesces from smallpox, is mocked by Lincoln's Inn Fields—"pleasant fields, where the sheep are all made into parchment, the goats into wigs, and the pasture into chaff." [1]

The two narratives in *Bleak House* reflect one another, and the multiplied characters and events of the novel are the thousand metamorphoses of a single reality. The ruined children and perverted families of Esther's story, like the anachronisms, stoppages, and false appearances exposed by the "author," are ironic variations on a single theme—the perversion of nature into not-nature. This theme is embodied in all the parts of the novel, down to the smallest descriptive details. Abstractions are suddenly brought to a kind of sickly life, as when Vholes tells Richard Carstone, "The suit does not sleep; we wake it up, we air it, we walk it about." The living and the non-living exchange attributes, roles, appearances: "You will have the goodness to make these materials into two members of parliament, and to send them home when done." Houses are transformed into their inhabitants, and transfixed again into stone, in a riot of animating and de-animating metaphors:

> It is a dull street under the best conditions; where the two long rows of houses stare at each other with that severity, that half-a-dozen of its greatest mansions seem to have been slowly stared into stone, rather than originally built in that material. It is a street of such dismal grandeur, so determined not to condescend to liveliness, that the doors and windows hold a gloomy state of their own in black paint and dust, and the echoing mews behind have a dry and massive appearance, as if they were

[1] For "pastoral" satire in *Bleak House,* see Louis Crompton, "Satire and Symbolism in *Bleak House," Nineteenth-Century Fiction,* XII (1958), 284–303.

reserved to stable the stone chargers of noble statues. Complicated garnish
of iron-work entwines itself over the flights of steps in this awful street;
and, from these petrified bowers, extinguishers for obsolete flambeaux
gasp at the upstart gas. (XLVIII)

This does not by any means exhaust Dickens' metamorphic ingenuity. In *Bleak House* the order of animal existences, a degeneration of
the human, is nearly as full as the human world. In Lincoln's Inn the
lawyers lie "like maggots in nuts," and in Tom-all-Alone's the poor
sleep in "maggot numbers." The Smallweeds are a whole bestiary of
monkeys, spiders, parrots, scorpions, toads, grubs, magpies, jackdaws,
pigs, and swine. Tulkinghorn is a "species of large rook." A distressingly large proportion of the animals live by preying on human life.
Vholes, the lawyer-serpent, spends half the book inch by inch ingesting
Richard Carstone, finishing him off with a final gulp. But the system
has, after all, its justification: "Make man-eating unlawful, and you
starve the Vholeses."

The perversion of nature which is expressed in the minutest details
and last elaborations of Dickens' style collects itself into larger and
larger aggregations and ascends to a coherence which rivals nature
itself. The elaborate motif linking Esther's experience, Chancery, the
fashionable world of the Dedlocks, and eventually seeming to involve
the whole of society, is that of a "system" superseding the system of
nature: "The fashionable world—tremendous orb, nearly five miles
round—is in full swing, and the solar system works respectfully at its
appointed distances. . . . It is morning in the great world; afternoon
according to the little sun" (XLVIII). When Gridley complains of his
treatment in an interminable Chancery suit which is driving him mad,
he is told that he " 'mustn't look to individuals. It's the system.' "
Richard Carstone, obsessed by his suit, suffers from "the careless spirit
of a gamester, who felt that he was part of a great gambling system."
The whole of society, in fact, may be conceived abstractly as a system.
Harold Skimpole considers that his "business in the social system is
to be agreeable. . . . It's a system of harmony." Sir Leicester Dedlock
thinks the "systematic" coherence of established customs, groups, and
so on is as necessary and fundamental as the coherence of the system
of nature, and at any change taking place in it he fears that " 'the floodgates of society are burst open, and the waters have—a—obliterated
the landmarks of the framework of the cohesion by which things are
held together.' " Finally Conversation Kenge masterfully sums up the
necessity for the system of equity:

"We are a great country, Mr. Jarndyce, we are a very great country. This
is a great system, Mr. Jarndyce, and would you wish a great country to
have a little system? No really, really!" He said this at the stair-head,
gently waving his right hand as if it were a silver trowel, with which to
spread the cement of his words on the structure of the system, and con-
solidate it for a thousand ages. (LXII)

This vision of the consolidation and persistence, through eons, of a
perverse organization competing with nature itself is one of the final
comments on the Jarndyce case, and the justification of the procedures
by which the suit has been carried to its ruinous conclusion. The only
weight *against* the system is thrown into the balance at the end of the
novel when Esther and Allan Woodcourt establish a center of "goodness" carrying on that of the original Bleak House. But only the *small*
area, it seems, is capable of salvation. Esther's goodness proves unable
to affect the massively intrenched "systematic" evil of whole classes
and professions. With Esther's marriage, we are perhaps permitted to
imagine that the seed of a new order has been sown, under the genial
supervision of the magician Jarndyce; but Chancery and the fashionable world, monsters of prehistory, remain unslain. Dickens, like
E. M. Forster, suggests that we are saved one by one, in our personal
relations, not in our generalized and abstract organizations. He seems
to deny that good *can* come from groups and organizations. It flows
only from the activity of individuals of superior sympathy and responsibility responding to other individuals.

The division of the story between Esther and an anonymous narrator segregates good from evil, and gives the good a specific locus—in
such people as Esther Summerson, and in Bleak House. Bleak House
is the fantastic and perhaps regressive retreat of the embattled saints
—the orphans and their benevolent protector. Richard Carstone, un
like Esther, abandons the Bleak House retreat, and scorns the protec-
tion of his guardian. Obsessed as he is by "Great Expectations," Richard's fate is controlled by the abstract mechanism of Chancery, and
by the parasites on it. The subject of his story is the destructive relation between an individual and a dehumanized social system of enormous extent and immovability. Esther survives, while Richard does
not. The difference in their fates results largely from the fact that
Richard throws himself into the destructive element, while Esther
keeps herself apart from it, refusing to submit herself to any organization, class, or abstract theory—whether it be Chancery, the fashionable world, or "telescopic" philanthropy. Esther's story and Richard's

are connected in being positive and negative "proofs" of the destructiveness of a corrupt and disorganized society.

Esther's part as an actor in the novel is relatively small. The world of *Bleak House* is too large and too scattered to be focussed on a single person. But as narrator she adds to the novel a center of "normal" consciousness, of emotional life and felt experience, which are necessary to define the abnormalities of the life and persons around her. In Esther, Dickens dramatizes the subject of all his novels: the struggle towards fulfillment of "natural" feelings in a world of abnormal, false, and cruel systems of belief, behavior, and human relationships. Esther's inner experience is the necessary complement of the author's entirely external ironic description. Without this "life" the elaborate satirical portrait of a disorganized society would be meaningless, or would lack what for Dickens is meaning—the fulfilled affective life of the individual. In dividing the story between two narrators Dickens has put a gulf between the self on one side, and public, organized, "bureaucratic" society on the other.

The double point of view in *Bleak House,* then, has its reasons. But it also has a very serious limitation. The limitation is in the quality of the consciousness Dickens has chosen as alternate narrator and representative of the self. Esther exists in the novel both as registering consciousness and as an ideal standard of moral values (the great ones being selflessness and energy in doing the duty which lies nearest). Other characters' admiring devotion to her is presented in her own narrative, not only through dialogue, but (and this is much more damaging) through her own summary. The result is that she appears to be convinced of her own saintliness, and to be at the greatest pains to dissemble her opinion. In failing to recognize that Esther's actions would in themselves communicate her virtue to us, without this coy self-consciousness, Dickens proves that he himself has not "realized" her character: he is evidently unable to *imagine* such selflessness as Esther's. Continuing to think longingly of her dolls, and accepting gratefully the "doll's house" (her own phrase) model of Bleak House into which John Jarndyce thrusts her with her new husband, Esther becomes a more insidious study of abnormal childhood than the overt study in the novel, Harold Skimpole. She becomes a particularly perverse and sentimental expression of Dickens' life-long over-valuation of the experience of the child. The ending of Esther's story, with its implied doctrine that our salvation requires us to be childish, is a sentimental and obviously inadequate solution to the serious moral and social problems Dickens raises.

At their most extreme divergence, the two points of view from which *Bleak House* is narrated—the sentimental and the ironic-satiric—are perhaps simply incompatible. The two narratives seem almost a product of schizophrenia, and *Bleak House* seems to be two novels: a melodramatic fairy-tale, and an extraordinarily bitter and inclusive social satire. What prevents this incompatibility from hopelessly splitting the novel is the fact that the solid core of *Bleak House* is dramatic action and speech—a center where the difference between the two narrators is slight. The energy and invention of *Bleak House* are in its satire. The power of the novel is not only in the "author's" elaborately ironic descriptions, but in the equally damning observations registered by Esther herself when her attention is not on herself or on her benevolent guardian—when she is neither moralizing nor sentimentalizing. Esther lacks the suppressed violence and underlined irony of the author-narrator, but she records, largely without comment, the same abnormalities that he does. The Pardiggles and Jellybys, Skimpole and Vholes of her experience are no less monstrous than the Tulkinghorn and Smallweeds of the other narrative, and what Esther sees in the elder Turveydrop is precisely what the anonymous observer, more wide-ranging, sees in the fashionable world as a whole. What is sentimental and self-righteous in Esther, then, is largely corrected by the whole context in which she exists. And this context is itself partly a product of her own observation. The insufficiencies of Dickens' view of her are absorbed into the complexity of the total structure of the novel.

The final unity of *Bleak House* is not so much one of plot (too many characters are irrelevant to what happens) or of point of view (the anonymous point of view sometimes undercuts Esther's) as of theme and satiric intention. In both Esther's and the author's narrative, nature (though it sometimes has its revenge) has everywhere been distorted—by system, mechanism, theory, degeneration into lower forms of life. This is the fact which is repeated and mirrored in the worlds and social strata and characters of *Bleak House*. Abstractly stated, the theme is nothing. In the totality of its concrete illustrations—treated comically, ironically, mysteriously, or portentously—it is magnificent. And the great instrument of the theme in *Bleak House* is the style. The style, more accurately, *is* the thorough penetration of every detail by the theme.

At the hands of a great artist, reality always undergoes a considerable transformation. Dickens' re-creation of reality is violent—as violent as Swift's, for example, in *Gulliver's Travels*. In both works, the violence of the distortion seems to measure the intensity of the satirist's feeling. In *Gulliver's Travels* the metamorphosis is achieved by transporting us into a different world, made fantastic by the changing of one or two fundamental facts, proportions, or "rules" of standard reality. Swift's effect is largely in the discrepancy between a fantastic world and the pedantic plausibility and the detailed matter-of-factness of the style in which it is described. Unlike Swift's, Dickens' changes are not in the very laws and ground of his world; his metamorphosis of reality is in the *details* of his world. Dickens' world is the everyday world distorted. Swift's is a fantasy world made plausible. Dickens works not only by suggestion, rhetorical device, wit, and tone, as Swift does, but by a much greater elaboration of mimicry and significant gesture. Sir Leicester speaks "as if he were nodding down at the man from a Mount," Conversation Kenge busily employs the "silver trowel" of his rhetoric, Chadband mouths a word often on his lips—"Terewth"—and narrative bursts into mimesis, concrete dramatic rendering.

The style of *Bleak House* is of course a *tour de force*. Its brilliance is forced on Dickens by the necessity of bringing his huge *dramatis personae* into some kind of order, of bridging the gap between the two voices of the novel, and of fusing the various forms of which the novel is composed. It is melodrama, fairy-tale, mystery, and satire, all at once. Each form subtly alters the others. The satire is hot and perspiring rather than cold and dry, and the irony is more melodramatic than dead-pan. In the anonymous narrative the fairy-tale has its ironic reflection, pastoral turns to satire, and mystery is treated comically and satirically. *Bleak House* turns back upon itself. Its elements are made to reflect upon and alter one another by a glittering virtuosity of style.

In the process, characters are stylized; they are distorted and reduced to the elements that are necessary to the expression of a single theme, and to the creation of a very emphatic concrete pattern. They become clusters of external signs ("poetically" repeated, as T. S. Eliot says). As in all Dickens' novels, most characters are reduced to characteristics, and this is the defect as well as the peculiar virtue of Dickens' characterization. This reduction fits perfectly the later, more satiric novels— particularly *Bleak House* and *Our Mutual Friend*—where it is intended to dehumanize the characters. In these later novels, "nature," except as a standard which is everywhere *implied,* tends to disappear, or to appear only intermittently, located in specific characters or places. This is the usual and perhaps the inevitable practice of satire. In the

interest of a more consistent texture, Dickens decisively distinguishes
scene and character (most characters) from "reality." The primary concern of the anonymous narrator in *Bleak House* is often with scene,
"background." From the background characters emerge. But they are
still part of the scene, done in its terms. (Both Chancery and Tulkinghorn, for example, are largely composed of dust.) Both characters and
scene are reduced to brief linguistic motifs which are amenable to
ironic or satiric or simply insistent repetition. The first description of
a character or scene is often elaborate, as in the first description of
Chancery or Chesney Wold or the nest of the Smallweeds. After the
first full description, Dickens selects significant images (Chancery's
mud, for example), gestures (Vholes's ingestion of Richard), or clichés
of speech (Chadband's "Terewth") to stand as brief signals of the person or scene. He creates his world by repetition and thematic development of these stylistic elements. He works *towards* the concentration of
metaphor or symbol. In later appearances of a setting or person, the
explanatory part of the initial description is suppressed. "As if" turns
into direct assertion; comparison becomes identity; simile develops into
metaphor. Sometimes the metamorphosis takes place in a single paragraph. Development is by repetition and by addition to the original
signs; and by repeating and varying motifs previously established (as
the fairy-tale motif of Bleak House is distorted in the Smallweeds, and
in Krook's role as ogre), Dickens achieves an increasing density of
meaning and internal connection. In *Bleak House* these stylistic devices serve the needs of concentration and identity within complexity.
It is an essential purpose of *Bleak House* to impress the image of chaos
on us, but the image itself escapes chaos; it is controlled and unified
by the style.

The Unpoetic Compromise

by G. Armour Craig

. . . The first narrative, in the conventional third person, connects for us at the outset the world of London and Chancery with the world of Fashion. The thick fog of the end of Michaelmas Term covers both: it reaches from the bored Lady Dedlock to the corrupted ground of a neglected city churchyard. Although no one can penetrate the fog of Chancery and no one can connect the ramifications of the great case of Jarndyce and Jarndyce, yet under the fog and darkness connections are constantly made. The impersonal narrator asks:

> What connexion can there be, between the place in Lincolnshire, the house in town, . . . and the whereabouts of Jo the outlaw with the broom, who had that distant ray of light upon him when he swept the churchyard steps? What connexion can there have been between many people in the innumerable histories of this world, who, from opposite sides of great gulfs, have nevertheless been very curiously brought together? (XVI)

And in his narrative such questions are answered. Jo the crossing-sweeper brings a mysterious lady to see the grave of the nameless law-writer whose hand Lady Dedlock has recognized. Lady Dedlock and the dead man are brought together across great gulfs by the curiosity of Tulkinghorn, the lawyer. And Esther Summerson is connected with Lady Dedlock by the curiosity of Mr. Guppy, the sentimental clerk with the authoritarian parent. Even Grandfather Smallweed connects Esther with Lady Dedlock in his curious association with The Reverend and Mrs. Chadband.

The second narrative, that of Esther Summerson, is in the first per-

"The Unpoetic Compromise: On the Relation Between Private Vision and Social Order in Nineteenth-Century English Fiction" by G. Armour Craig. From Society and Self in the Novel, *English Institute Essays* (New York: Columbia University Press, 1955), pp. 41–50. Copyright © 1956 by Columbia University Press. Reprinted by permission of the publisher.

son, and it opens with the assertion: "I know I am not clever" (III). The connections made in the third-person narrative are incomprehensible to Esther. She cannot understand the stigma which is her aunt's sole contribution to her education: "Your mother, Esther, was your disgrace, and you are hers" (III). She is the subject of investigations and concealments described in the third-person narrative, but she is apart from them. But though she is not clever, Esther is good, and by her direct, inarticulate humanity she crosses some gulfs. When Mrs. Pardiggle's bristling inquisition succeeds only in setting up an "iron barrier" between her message of grace and the poor brickmakers of St. Albans, Esther, weeping compassion, shares the sorrows of Jenny, the mistreated mother. When Jo the crossing-sweeper comes in his sickness to the brickmakers', having been "moved on" and "chivvied" by Inspector Buckct, Mr. Chadband, Mrs. Snagsby, and other seekers of connection, Esther cannot know that he is surprised and frightened by her because she resembles the lady he has taken to see the "berryin ground." But she can take Jo to Bleak House and give him medicine and care. She risks disease, as that believer in the harmonious fitness of things, Harold Skimpole, will not. And from Charley, her maid, who nurses Jo and whom she in turn nurses, Esther takes the fever. Its effects change her face.

The judicious reader, if he will, may see Esther's disease and disfigurement as an illustration of a large theme first adumbrated in *Dombey and Son*. There, in a solemn declamation on the origin of evil, Dickens proposes an analogy: "men of science," he says, report that from the "polluted air" of the slums of cities there rise "noxious particles" which if they were visible would appear "lowering in a dense black cloud . . . and rolling slowly on to corrupt the better portions of a town." "But," says the prophetic voice, "if the moral pestilence that rises with them, and in the eternal laws of outraged Nature, is inseparable from them, could be made discernible too, how terrible the revelation! Then we should see depravity, impiety, drunkenness, theft, murder, and a long train of nameless sins against the natural affections and repulsions of mankind, . . . creeping on, to blight the innocent and spread contagion among the pure." Esther's fever of course has its origin in the "polluted air" of the worst part of the city; though the "noxious particles" of its "corruption" are invisible, we can trace their movement. Jo has come from Tom-all-Alone's, the decaying property at issue in the great Chancery suit. And Jo has also come from the pestilential churchyard where Esther's nameless father is buried. The course of the physical pestilence, from the church-yard to Jo to Charley to Esther, is clear. But the "moral pestilence," the "creeping on" of literally "nameless sins" that "blight the innocent," is not so easily discernible. Perhaps the apt illustration is the dwindling away of Richard Carstone, who succumbs to the wasting fever of Chancery. But the causes of Richard's corruption are described in the third-person narrative; only its piteous effects are wept over by Esther. And the blight of Richard of course involves no typhoid or cholera literally rising from the wastelands of the city.

There is no necessity, it is true, that the theme announced in *Dombey* should be expressed in *Bleak House*. Yet to notice its partial apposite-ness to the account of Esther's illness is to notice also how removed she is from even the connections and inseparabilities decreed by "out-raged Nature." In her illness Esther becomes temporarily blind, and if we read her distress as the outcome of the moral stigma announced by her aunt we shall be puzzled by its aftermath. For the fever so trans-forms her face that no one henceforth can connect her with Lady Dedlock. Indeed, after her illness, Esther meets her long-lost mother at Chesney Wold, and it is difficult to imagine a more self-effacing re-sponse to Lady Dedlock's revelation: Esther says, "I felt, through all my tumult of emotion, a burst of gratitude to the providence of God that I was so changed as that I never could disgrace her by any trace of likeness; as that nobody could ever now look at me, and look at her, and remotely think of any near tie between us" (XXXVI). Esther's world is impenetrable to those who look for "ties" near or remote. Next day, after thinking in vain upon the story her mother has told—"I could not disentangle all that was about me"—Esther meets her friend and fellow-ward, Ada, for the first time since her transformation. "Ah, my angel girl! the old dear look, all love, all kindness, all affection. Nothing else in it—no, nothing, nothing!" (XXXVI). Esther is safe in her world of goodness and affection.

Between the narrative of Esther and the narrative in which Krook, the parody of the Lord Chancellor, spontaneously combusts in his rag-and-bottle shop surrounded by secrets he cannot decipher, the gulf is greater than can be bridged by any connection. Dickens has cast Esther's narrative in the past tense; the third-person narrative is all in the present tense. Krook's charred remains are discovered before our eyes; the savor of his decomposition presently fills the neighborhood and mingles with the fog. Esther, moreover, as an independent narra-tor, is never a character in the impersonal narrative: she appears there

but once and by report only, when Jo on his deathbed tells Mr.
Snagsby that "the lady as wos and yit as warn't the t'other lady" has
come to visit him (XLVII). Mr. Jarndyce, who alone rivals Esther in
goodness, also appears but once in the third-person narrative, again
virtually by report and at Jo's deathbed. Skimpole, the Pardiggles and
Jellybys—all the grotesques of charity and goodwill—appear only in
Esther's narrative. She never meets Sir Leicester Dedlock, though early
in her narrative she innocently encounters Krook, and near the end
she is puzzled to see Grandfather Smallweed. It is perhaps irrelevant
to systematize the division of roles between the two narratives, and
Dickens occasionally attributes to Esther an observation inappropriate
for her. But it is as clear as grammar and structure can make it that the
voice of the impersonal narrator cannot appear in Esther's narrative,
and the converse, I think, holds as well.

The difference between the two narratives is most nearly removed
in the episode of Lady Dedlock's flight. Threatened by Tulkinghorn,
who knows her secret, Lady Dedlock disappears. The search for her is
conducted by Inspector Bucket, who, along with Allan Woodcourt, the
doctor, seems to be the new social mind capable of any connection.
The search is narrated by Esther, to whom the pausing and speeding,
the dashing out of London and the doubling back, are bewildering.
The pursuit ends at the entrance to the churchyard: "a dreadful spot
in which the night was very slowly stirring; but where I could see heaps
of dishonoured graves and stones, hemmed in by filthy houses, with a
few dull lights in their windows, and on these walls a thick humidity
broke out like a disease." Here are the pestilential darkness and
miasma kept constantly before us in the third-person narrative. And
here too, we may expect, is that gradual lifting of the night, that clear-
ing of the prospect, in which Esther takes pleasure as her first morning dawns at Bleak House. Here, if anywhere, in the faintly stirring
night, and before her father's grave, Esther will make the great connection. For at the entrance to the cemetery, "drenched in the fearful
wet of such a place," is a woman lying. "I saw before me, lying on the
step, the mother of the dead child. She lay there, with one arm around
a bar of the iron gate, and seeming to embrace it." Esther thinks the
woman is Jenny, the poor brickmaker's wife whose dead child she
covered with her own handkerchief. Bucket tries to suggest to her
another connection; he tells her that Lady Dedlock changed clothes
with Jenny, and that Jenny went on to mislead the pursuers. But Esther
cannot understand him: "They changed clothes at the cottage. I could

repeat the words in my mind, and I knew what they meant of themselves; but I attached no meaning to them in any other connexion."
She sees Woodcourt restrain Bucket, a look of compassion on his face.
"But my understanding for all this was gone." She has seen "a dis-
tressed, unsheltered, senseless creature," and goes to her. "I passed on
to the gate, and stooped down. I lifted the heavy head, put the long
dank hair aside, and turned the face. And it was my mother cold and
dead." Esther, at last, has seen everything.

But just here is the end of Chapter LIX of *Bleak House*. Chapter LX
begins, "I proceed to other passages of my narrative." And after a
sentence or two about the consolation "from the goodness all about
me," Esther moves on to the account of her own little Bleak House in
the north with Allan Woodcourt, to the hilarious collapse of the great
lawsuit, to the sad exit of Richard Carstone, and to the last delicious
assurance: "I know that my dearest little pets are very pretty, and
that my darling is very beautiful, and that my husband is very handsome, and that my guardian has the brightest and most benevolent face
that was ever seen; and that they can very well do without much beauty
in me—even supposing—" Some readers may wince at so rosy a sunset, but it is the proper last word for Esther.

For it is as clear as the blank space of a chapter division that the
great connection is not to be made in her gentle language. As she approaches the figure on the step, her terms are consistent: "my understanding for all this was gone"; "I could repeat the words in my mind
. . . but I attached no meaning to them in any other connexion." She
not only cannot understand the change of clothes and the erratic journey through the night; there are also no words in her narrative to
express the meaning of her final discovery. It may be that Esther is
herself in a sense "the dead child" and that her recognition of the
fallen woman as "the mother of the dead child" is some very fine
writing indeed. Yet to say so is to insist by her symbolic death upon the
remoteness of Esther from the ties that would bind the severed halves
of this enormous book. The two narratives are as separate as their
grammar, and if the separation is a flaw, it seems to me a flaw which
only a great writer could have committed. It is sometimes a sign of
genius not to follow ideas to their conclusions, not to bring them all
into harmony, and the genius of Dickens here is his recognition that
while two narratives are necessary they are not combinable. The voice
that would articulate both is far on the other side of silence.

The sermon on moral and physical pestilence in *Dombey and Son* is concluded by an apostrophe: "Oh for a good spirit who would take the housetops off . . . and show a Christian people what dark shapes issue from amidst their homes . . . For only one night's view of the pale phantoms rising . . . from the thick and sullen air where Vice and Fever propagate together, raining down tremendous social retributions. . . . Bright and blest the morning that should rise on such a night . . ." However angelic she may be, Esther Summerson has no such dimensions as these. The "bright, blest morning" rises on her own night, not on that of all London and all society. The reader may know in the critical scene that the humid graveyard contains both her father and her mother, but he will have to strain a little to see that Vice and Fever have rained down their retribution here. Lady Dedlock dies of exposure, but whether in necessary compensation for the sins of her youth or in pathetic wastefulness of innocence, we do not know. We know only that Esther is good, is kind, and runs to the figure on the stones precisely because she does not understand. She does not know the world in terms of poverty or vice or degradation; she knows, what the Mrs. Pardiggles and Lord Chancellors do not, only Jenny, the mother of the dead child.

The goodness of this "I" cannot engulf the world of *Bleak House*; it cannot dissipate the fog or dry up the pestilence of the city. On the one hand, spontaneous combustion: the evils of society will explode of themselves if no Angel comes to expose them. This is no doubt a naïve faith, and certainly Dickens has his troubles with it. But on the other hand, goodness, sympathy, love, affection, the satisfactions of the private vision. It is their staying on the other hand that is so impressive here. Though he may have hoped for the self-destruction of the institutions he condemned, Dickens was neither so foolish nor so cruel as to conceive of the end of the world in a blood-bath of love and kindness. The voice of "outraged Nature" or of the spirit above the housetops must speak in tones louder than those of a not very clever "I." In *Bleak House* Dickens rejected the ruthless shape of fantasy for the unpoetic compromise of two parallel and unmeeting narrative lines. It would require the style of Henry James and a heroine as loftily placed as Milly Theale to bring them together. But that is another and a longer story.

Religious Folly

by Mark Spilka

Both Dickens and Kafka began their adult careers in law. After leaving school, Dickens worked as an office boy for lawyers, then turned to law reporting in Doctors' Commons. These legal cloisters lay in a shady nook beside St. Paul's; the courts were ecclesiastical, and, for Dickens, the courtroom seemed like a chapel where "monkish attorneys" muddled wills and testaments. Kafka studied the law directly, took his doctorate in 1906, then served his year of clerkship.[1] In *Bleak House* and *The Trial,* both writers fashioned oddly religious Courts, and used them to exemplify the adult world; and again there are signs that Kafka followed Dickens' lead. Admittedly, Kafka himself makes no remarks on *Bleak House*; it does not appear among his books, and none of his friends record it in his reading. Yet, as Rudolf Vašata observes:

> The similarity between *The Trial* and *Bleak House* is obvious. . . . The central theme of both novels is the machinery of law crushing everybody and everything which comes under its wheels, the victim realising all its horrors without understanding its mechanism. And it is equally obvious that, in both cases, the legal system and its workings are used merely as a symbol for the society which they are serving.[2]

Vašata's insistence on the social parallel seems arbitrary and exclusive. One might agree more readily with George Ford, that "Kafka is

"Religious Folly." From Dickens and Kafka *by Mark Spilka (Bloomington, Ind.: Indiana University Press, 1963), pp. 199–210. Copyright © 1963 by Indiana University Press. Reprinted by permission of the publisher.*

[1] Edgar Johnson, *Charles Dickens: His Tragedy and Triumph* (New York: Simon and Schuster, 1952), Vol. I, pp. 51–2, 57–8; Max Brod, *Franz Kafka: A Biography,* trans. G. Humphrey Roberts (New York: Schocken, 1947), p. 78.

[2] Rudolf Vašata, "*Amerika* and Charles Dickens," *The Kafka Problem,* ed. Angel Flores (New York: New Directions, 1946), p. 135. For another source for *The Trial,* see Philip Rahv, "The Death of Ivan Ilyich and Joseph K.," *Image and Idea,* pp. 121–139. Tolstoy's hero, a law official with a mysterious wound, leads a pointless bourgeois life, like Joseph K.; but he is not crushed by the machinery of the law, nor is the law conceived in pseudo-religious terms, as in Dickens' novel.

primarily concerned with the apparent muddle of Divine Law, and Dickens with the actual muddle of human law." [3] Or one might even go beyond this, to suggest that Dickens gives a pseudo-religious cast to the law which magnifies its horrors. But whatever its form, the legal metaphor is central in both novels, and the similarity between them is decidedly strong. When it comes to point of view, moreover, a more subtle relation develops than either Ford or Vašata suggests. Consider the legal scheme in *Bleak House* as it appears to children. A pseudo-religious Court would appeal to Kafka, but a childhood view of that Court, especially the view of Esther Summerson, the outcast Jo, and the desperate litigant Richard Carstone, would appeal with striking force. For children lack a comprehensive grasp of complicated systems; they convert their complexities into immediate effects of absurdity and confusion; they respond, as it were, from below, with emotional immediacy and concreteness, but without those speculative and synthetic powers which make for clarity, scope and fullness of perception: and Kafka, for all his intellectual sophistication, for all his legalistic and Talmudic sense of contradictions and alternatives, was as confined as Dickens by the child's emotional outlook. By following up these figures, then, we can perhaps explain how *Bleak House* might have influenced *The Trial* or, at the least, prefigured its appearance; in either case, the important fact is continuity of vision.

First, Esther Summerson. Like Pip and David Copperfield, she tells her portion of the novel directly, while Dickens covers the broader scene in alternating chapters. Through these narrative shifts the author presents his theme from two perspectives. With Dickens we view the fogs of Chancery from above, with ironic severity; with Esther we see them from within, as a sensitive and tender child might see them, or more accurately, a woman reviewing youth and childhood. Esther's name suggests her narrative function: she is the "summer sun," a bright, sustaining force for those around her, in contrast to the darkening blight of Chancery. Unfortunately, she seems colorless and dull in the middle chapters, though radiant enough in describing childhood and her later pursuit of a sinful mother. For Esther is an illegitimate child, a shameful outcast, and seems able to speak best of matters which resemble Dickens' life. Her godmother, Miss Barbary, is a severely religious woman who treats her as a pariah, suppresses the facts of her parentage,

[3] George Ford, *Dickens and His Readers* (Princeton University Press, 1955), pp. 255-256.

and keeps her away from other children. In consequence, her birthdays are always glum occasions. Dickens himself was sent to the warehouse on his twelfth birthday,[4] and Esther receives a similar shock on hers. Frightened by her godmother's somber face, which seems to imply her guilt in being born, she forces her to speak out plainly:

> "Your mother, Esther, is your disgrace, and you were hers. . . . Unfortunate girl, orphaned and degraded from the first of these evil anniversaries, pray daily that the sins of others be not visited upon your head, according to what is written. . . .
>
> "Submission, self-denial, diligent work, are the preparation for a life begun with such a shadow on it. You are different from other children, Esther, because you were not born, like them, in common sinfulness and wrath. You are set apart." (III)

So too was Dickens "set apart" and forced to do hard, depleting labor. Accordingly, he could invest these scenes with deepfelt needs, or with characteristic emblems for those needs, like Esther's doll, which carries the psychic charge of Barkis' box, Cuttle's hat, or Miss Mowcher's ambulant umbrella. Esther begins her story, for instance, by mentioning her lonely talks with "Dolly," who faithfully waits her return from school each day and listens to her account of childhood woes. The doll replaces the missing mother here, and provides the girl with her only source of comfort. Thus, when Esther learns of her disgraceful birth, she runs to her room, holds "that solitary friend" against her bosom, and repeats the story of her birthday:

> I . . . confided to her that I would try, as hard as ever I could, to repair the fault I had been born with (of which I confessedly felt guilty and yet innocent), and would strive as I grew up to be industrious, contented, and kind-hearted, and to do some good to some one, and win some love to myself if I could. (III)

Two years later Esther is able to win herself some love. Her godmother dies, and she is sent by an unknown guardian to a boarding school, where she speedily wins the hearts of all around her. Before leaving for school, however, she wraps her doll in a shawl ("I am half ashamed to tell it") and buries her in the garden below her window. About six years afterwards, she receives a comic proposal from the bumptious Mr. Guppy, one of the law clerks from Kenge and Carboy, which stirs up painful memories: she again goes to her room, begins

---

[4] Jack Lindsay, *Charles Dickens: A Biographical and Critical Study* (London: Andrew Dakers, 1930), p. 50.

to laugh and cry, and feels "as if an old chord had been more coarsely touched than it ever had been since the days of the dear old doll, long buried in the garden" (IX). So the doll is strongly connected with the absence, on the one hand, of a mother's love, and with marriage on the other. It suggests the sense of exclusion and inadequacy, or of dreams gone wrong, which Dickens himself might have felt in these connections, and which he seems to associate with the search for love.

At twenty Esther is called to her guardian's house to serve as governess to an adopted ward. When she arrives in London, the city is so full of dense brown smoke (the fog of Chancery) that Esther feels bewildered:

> We drove slowly through the dirtiest and darkest streets that ever were seen in the world (I thought), and in such a distracting state of confusion that I wondered how the people kept their senses, until we passed into sudden quietude under an old gateway, and drove on through a silent square until we came to an odd nook in a corner, where there was an entrance up a steep, broad flight of stairs, like an entrance to a church. And there really was a churchyard, outside under some cloisters, for I saw the gravestones from the staircase window. (III)

The converted church (for what else can we call it?) is Kenge and Carboy's law office. In the same location, but around the corner, under a colonnade, and in at a side door, is the Lord High Chancellor's office, where Esther meets the wards in Chancery, Miss Ada Clare and her cousin Richard Carstone. All three of them are orphans; all meet together, for the first time, before a roaring fire in the outer room; and together all face his lordship, who sits in an armchair in the next room, dressed in black. Esther is touched that this dry official place is "home" for the lovely Ada: "The Lord High Chancellor, at his best, appeared so poor a substitute for the love and pride of parents." Esther herself is supposedly "not related to any party in the cause"; but she is actually related to the cause, illegitimately, through her mother, Lady Dedlock, and perhaps to the parties in it too, since Richard Carstone is allied to Lady Dedlock "by remote consanguinity." Thus the three young people —Ada, Richard and Esther—really stand together as wards of the court; their "father" is the Lord High Chancellor; and just as Ada is later called a "child of the universe," so are they all "children of the universe." At present they are baffled by the events which bring them to the Chancellor's office. But before they leave, their bafflement turns to sudden alarm:

We looked at one another, half laughing at our being like the children in the wood, when a curious little old woman in a squeezed bonnet, and carrying a reticule, came curtseying and smiling up to us, with an air of great ceremony.

"O!" said she. "The wards in Jarndyce! Very happy, I am sure, to have the honour! It is a good omen for youth, and hope, and beauty, when they find themselves in this place, and don't know what's to come of it."

"Mad!" whispered Richard, not thinking she could hear him.

"Right! Mad, young gentleman," she returned so quickly that he was quite abashed. "I was a ward myself. I was not mad at that time," curtseying low, and smiling between every little sentence. "I had youth, and hope. I believe, beauty. It matters very little now. Neither of the three served, or saved me. I have the honour to attend Court regularly. With my documents. I expect a judgment. Shortly. On the Day of Judgment." (III)

The little madwoman is Miss Flite. Along with the frenzied Mr. Gridley, who later dies through defending his legal interest, she represents the fate of Richard Carstone, and of all other wards in Chancery who would assert their claims before the Court. Through such hints, alarms and portents, Dickens gives a religious cast to the law in *Bleak House*. In a single chapter, his heroine is first impressed with her sinfulness, then plunged through a squalid urban scene to reach a church-like nook in a quiet square; soon she stands, along with other children of the universe, before the Lord High Chancellor, their common "father"—and afterwards receives a hint of Judgment Day. To her the world *appears* to be very like the world which Kafka's heroes actually inhabit. Indeed, her guardian, John Jarndyce, is involved in a lawsuit which suggests a number of Kafkan metaphors, like the punishment scheme in "The Penal Colony" or the unfinished wall in "The Great Wall of China":

A certain Jarndyce, in an evil hour, made a great fortune, and made a great Will. In the question how the trusts under that Will are to be administered, the fortune left by the Will is squandered away; the legatees under the Will are reduced to such a miserable condition that they would be sufficiently punished, if they had committed an enormous crime in having money left them; and the Will itself is made a dead letter. . . . And thus, through years and years, and lives and lives, everything goes on, constantly beginning over and over again, and nothing ever ends. And we can't get out of the suit on any terms, for we are made parties to it, and *must be* parties to it, whether we like it or not. (VIII)

So the three orphans and their guardian are involved in a legal muddle which suggests Original Sin. Even Ada senses this, as she speaks of herself as the enemy of "a great number of relations and others," who are also her enemies, all "ruining one another, without knowing how or why, . . . in constant doubt and discord all our lives. It seems very strange, as there must be right somewhere, that an honest judge in real earnest has not been able to find out through all these years where it is" (V). Ada says this as the orphans leave the dark and airless apartment of Miss Flite, which is located above an old rag and bottle warehouse. The owner of the warehouse, Mr. Krook, is called the Lord Chancellor by his neighbors. His shop is called the Court of Chancery, because of the tremendous collection of old ink bottles, law books and legal papers hoarded there. Krook admits to the comparison ("We both grub on in a muddle"), and his congested shop, which is located in the squalid district around the Court, suggests the pervasiveness of the legal blight. It also helps to reveal the inner nature of the system, through the corruptness of Krook and the bleak, hopeless lives of his tenants, in the dark rooms above.

In *The Trial* the artist's garret performs a similar function. Like Kafka's supernatural Court, it is located in a dirty tenement house, though in another section of town; yet it is directly connected with law offices, as if the entire city were a sprawling Court, constantly in session, even in the most unexpected places, and sitting in perpetual judgment on Joseph K. On the stairs leading up to the garret, moreover, there are leering adolescent girls who "belong to the Court" (*T*, p. 189). K. has already run into flocks of children in the tenement where his first interrogation is held, and the woman who then directs him to the courtroom is washing children's clothes. Scenes like these play an important part in *Bleak House*. At Mrs. Jellyby's, children sprawl about the house in a welter of confusion, falling down stairs, getting their heads stuck through the outer railings, pushing their faces into the orphans' bedroom. In the country, at the cottage of a poor family, five children have died and a sixth succumbs at Ada's touch. Near the Court itself, three orphans are locked in a cold, barren room, while their adolescent sister takes in washing to support them. Their father, recently dead, has been connected with the Court in a minor capacity, and this connection suggests what is true of all these children: they are all wards in Chancery, either as victims of social neglect and commercial hardheartedness, or of the false and ineffectual

philanthropy of the middle class. For in *Bleak House,* as in *The Trial,*
"everything belongs to the Court"; in fact, life even *begins* under its
jurisdiction.

As many critics remark, the legal metaphor extends to social, economic and political realms, in *Bleak House,* from the rich manor at
Chesney Wold through the muddle of Parliament and of the commercial middle class, down to the crashing tenements in Tom-all-
Alone's. More pertinently, it also extends to sexual realms, though
always in connection with the social problem. George Santayana notes,
for example, that Lady Dedlock's secret is treated "as if it were the sin
of Adam, remote, mysterious, inexpiable." [5] In terms of dramatic
tension, this means that the whole novel is grounded in socio-sexual
mystery—or in the sin of Lady Dedlock and Captain Hawdon, of which
Esther is the illegitimate fruit. From Esther's childhood guilt through
Hawdon's mysterious death to Lady Dedlock's fatal collapse in the
snow, the sexual crime informs the social muddle and provides it with
a personal context. Hence Edmund Wilson's comment:

> At the bottom of the whole gloomy edifice is the body of Lady Dedlock's
> lover and Esther Summerson's father, Captain Hawdon, the reckless sol-
> dier, adored by his men, beloved by women, the image of the old life-
> loving England, whose epitaph Dickens is now writing. Captain Hawdon
> has failed in that world, has perished as a friendless and penniless man,
> and has been buried in the pauper's graveyard in one of the foulest quar-
> ters of London, but the loyalties felt for him by the living will endure
> and prove so strong, after his death, that they will pull that world apart.[6]

Lady Dedlock's crime, then, is to betray Hawdon's love (and by that
act, to betray the lower classes) by marrying for social position. Yet
their common crime is illicit love, which Dickens treats as the sin of
Adam. Thus, as Hawdon dies, he lies above Krook's shop in a dark,
foul, filthy room, the shutters of which are pierced by two gaunt holes,
resembling giant staring eyes. Dickens calls them the eyes of famine,
but Hawdon's immediate death is caused by opium, a drug which
Dickens elsewhere connects with sexual passion.[7] If these giant eyes
admonish sexual as well as social crimes, then the scene combines some

---

[5] George Santayana, "Dickens," *Soliloquies in England* (New York: Scribner's,
1923), p. 61.
[6] Edmund Wilson, "Dickens: The Two Scrooges," *Eight Essays* (New York:
Doubleday, 1954), p. 42.
[7] See *The Mystery of Edwin Drood,* where John Jasper's opium dreams are connected with dancing girls, and with his passionate desire to possess Rosa Bud.

of the harshest memories of Dickens' past with growing marital tensions. He seems to align himself with Hawdon here: he too had been rejected, by the family of Maria Beadnell, for lack of money and social position; and as Edmund Wilson observes, he too had spent his life without any clear-cut social rank, a member of no respectable class, and an enemy of all fashionable pomp and snobbery. But more than this, he was on the verge of experiments in sexual license, along with his young friend Wilkie Collins, which were foreign to his nature. In Hawdon's betrayal of the moral code he seems to convict himself of real or impending lapses. His sense of guilt and inadequacy, which began with the warehouse episode and which was deepened by the Beadnell fiasco, is now connected with forbidden love.

Kafka may have sensed this element in *Bleak House*. He seems to borrow the staring eyes, for example, when Joseph K. and his uncle visit Advocate Huld "in the very suburb where the Law Court had its attic offices":

> Behind a grille in the door two great dark eyes appeared, gazed at the two visitors for a moment, and then vanished again; yet the door did not open. K. and his uncle assured each other that they had really seen a pair of eyes. "A new maid, probably afraid of strangers," said K.'s uncle and knocked again. Once more the eyes appeared and now they seemed almost somber, yet that might have been an illusion created by the naked gas-jet which burned just over their heads and kept hissing shrilly but gave little light. "Open the door!" shouted K.'s uncle, banging upon it with his fists, "we're friends of the Herr Advocate's." "The Herr Advocate is ill," came a whisper from behind them. A door had opened at the other end of the little passage and a man in a dressing-gown was standing there imparting this information in a hushed voice.

When the door is finally opened, K. recognizes the dark protuberant eyes in the girl Leni, with whom he later makes love, to the detriment of his case before the Court. Now Leni stands in the entrance hall with a candle in her hand:

> "The Herr Advocate is ill," said the girl, as K.'s uncle without any hesitation, made towards an inner door. . . . "Is it his heart?" [he asked]. "I think so," said the girl, she had now found time to precede him with the candle and open the door of a room. In one corner, which the candlelight had not yet reached, a face with a long beard attached rose from a pillow. (pp. 125–126)

Compare this with the scene in *Bleak House* where the aged lawyer, Tulkinghorn, who is the legal representative for Lady Dedlock's husband, enters Hawdon's room. When he comes to the dark door, he "knocks, receives no answer, opens it, and accidentally extinguishes his candle." On a low bed opposite the fire, "a confusion of dirty patch-work, lean-ribbed ticking, and coarse sacking," he sees a spectral bearded figure. Crying "Hallo," he rattles on the door and strikes it with his iron candle-stick. The candle in the room goes out, "and leaves him in the dark; with the gaunt eyes in the shutters staring down upon the bed." A touch from behind makes the lawyer start; Krook whispers in his ear, and the two go in together, whispering, after Krook returns with a lighted candle. "As the light goes in, the great eyes in the shutters, darkening, seem to close. Not so the eyes upon the bed" (X–XI).

In the turmoil which follows, a young surgeon, Allan Woodcourt, appears suddenly on one side of Hawdon's bed, as if from nowhere (even as Inspector Bucket will materialize, more auspiciously, in a later scene).[8] On the other side stands Krook, the mock High Chancel-lor, while the lawyer Tulkinghorn stands silently in the background, near an old portmanteau. In *The Trial,* as K. and his uncle converse with the ailing Advocate, a form begins to stir in a dark corner of the room, and the Chief Clerk of the Court appears there, at a little table. Mood, theme and arrangement are thus similar in each scene: there

[8] Woodcourt appears, unannounced, as "a dark young man" who speaks from "the other side of the bed" in the general turmoil. Mr. Bucket's materialization in lawyer Tulkinghorn's rooms is more dramatic:

> Mr. Snagsby is dismayed to see, standing with an attentive face between him-self and the lawyer, at a little distance from the table, a person with a hat and stick in his hand, who was not there when he himself came in, and has not since entered by the door or by either of the windows. There is a press in the room, but its hinges have not creaked, nor has a step been audible upon the floor. Yet this third person stands there . . . a composed and quiet listener. He is a stoutly built, steady-looking, sharp-eyed man in black, of about the middle-age. . . . There is nothing remarkable about him at first sight but his ghostly manner of appearing. (XXII)

Compare the Chief Clerk's appearance in *The Trial,* as the ailing Advocate speaks:

> "Of course I'm somewhat handicapped now because of my illness, but in spite of that good friends of mine from the Law Courts visit me now and then. . . . For example there's a dear friend of mine visiting me at this very moment," and he waved a hand towards a dark corner of the room. "Where?" asked K., almost roughly, in his first shock of astonishment. He looked round uncertainly; the light of the small candle did not nearly reach the opposite wall. And then some form or other in the dark corner actually began to stir. By the light of the candle, which his uncle now held high above his head, K. could see an elderly gentleman sitting there at a little table. He must have been sitting without even drawing breath, to have remained for so long unnoticed. (p. 131)

are mysterious staring eyes, to suggest the sin of Adam; there are loud rappings at the door, hushed voices, and sudden interruptions from behind; there are sickbeds and legal figures in faltering candlelight, and dark forms which materialize from nowhere; and finally, there is a mock or substitute Chancellor from the Court, to lend an air of judgment to the entire tableau. The parallels run rather thick for mere coincidence.

If the expiation theme appealed to Kafka, he might have liked its superbly-told completion, in the final chapters, where Lady Dedlock pays for her share in sexual crime. Stricken by guilt, she has approached her daughter humbly, embraced her for the first and last time, and asked her forgiveness. She believes, however, that she has earned her "earthly punishment" and must bear it. When Tulkinghorn, the legal keeper of aristocratic secrets, is murdered, her husband learns of her sexual sins, and the house of Dedlock falls. Aware of her exposure, and falsely accused of murder, she flees the house on foot, pursued by Esther and Inspector Bucket with a futile message of forgiveness. Here Esther re-emerges, with renewed vitality, as an innocent point of view in a darkened world. Her dreamlike account of the search through squalid urban scenes, along snow-filled country roads, then back again to Chancery Lane, becomes a psychological journey in which houses put on human shapes and water-gates close and open in her mind. The journey ends at her father's grave, where her mother lies dead, dressed in the garb of the poor, the class she had deserted. In Kafka's novel, *Amerika*, another illegitimate child, the servant girl Therese (whose name resembles Esther's), tells of her mother's death in dreamlike fashion a self-inflicted death involving sexual and economic betrayal and wanderings through urban streets in winter. The parallel seems worth mentioning, since it helps to establish Kafka's possible interest in this sequence, where the sin of Adam gives tension and significance to the legal metaphor.[9]

[9] Therese's story differs circumstantially from Esther's. Her mother is a poor immigrant whose lover, a foreman mason, has sent for her and the child from America. When they arrive he soon deserts them, and the mother takes her life at a building site. Therese herself is only a girl of five, and she accompanies (rather than pursues) her mother on her journey. Perhaps she descends from Dickens' Nell (in *The Old Curiosity Shop*) through Dostoevsky's Nellie (in *The Insulted and Injured*), another illegitimate child who walks through wintry streets with a dying mother. The imitation may be twice-removed; yet as E. W. Tedlock observes, Therese's story, "in its quality of grotesquely pathetic pantomime, is straight Dickens." If so, it may derive from *Bleak House*, at least in theme (sexual and economic betrayal) and texture.

Bleak House

by J. Hillis Miller

It is a dull street under the best conditions; where the two long rows of houses stare at each other with that severity, that half-a-dozen of its greatest mansions seem to have been slowly stared into stone, rather than originally built in that material. (XLVIII)

The Temple, Chancery Lane, Serjeants' Inn, and Lincoln's Inn even unto the Fields, are like tidal harbours at low water; where stranded proceedings, offices at anchor, idle clerks lounging on lopsided stools that will not recover their perpendicular until the current of Term sets in, lie high and dry upon the ooze of the long vacation. (XIX)

Though the world of *Bleak House* is not, we discover, the sheer atomistic chaos it at first appears to be, the connection, by repetition, of successive moments in isolated locations does not organize this chaos. It does not seem that a truly human existence is possible here—no organization of time into a lived duration, no relation between people making possible significant communication. But we come to see that the inhuman fixity and paralysis which seems to possess things and men in *Bleak House* is not a permanent condition. It is not now in the same stasis it has always maintained. The houses were not originally stone. They were "slowly stared into stone." And the ooze and idleness of the long vacation is merely the motionless end point of a progressive withdrawal of the tide of human action and life. Prior to the timeless paralysis of things there was a long process of deceleration and decay. It is impossible to stop the forward movement of things in time. Both an attempt to freeze the present as a repetition of a past time and the eternally repeated moment of expectation which awaits some definitive event in the future are essentially a denial of the proper human relation to time and to the objective world. Both are cut off from the

"Bleak House." *From* Charles Dickens: The World of His Novels *by J. Hillis Miller (Cambridge, Mass.: Harvard University Press, 1958), pp. 190–205. Copyright © 1958 by the President and Fellows of Harvard College. Reprinted by permission of the publisher.*

"moving age." But man cannot cut himself off from time and the world. If he is not related authentically to them, if he does not command them, they will command him. He will be assimilated into the inhuman world and become part of a mechanical concatenation of causes and effects which is a horrible parody of historical continuity. In the absence of human intervention things will take matters into their own hands, and initiate a long natural process of decay and disintegration in which man will become unwittingly involved. The world possesses an immanent tendency toward decomposition which only the most delicately and resolutely applied constructive force can counteract. And it is just this force which is almost totally absent in *Bleak House*.

The world of the novel is already, when the story begins, a kind of junk heap of broken things. This is especially apparent in the great number of disorderly, dirty, broken-down interiors in the novel. The Jellyby household is "nothing but bills, dirt, waste, noise, tumbles down-stairs, confusion, and wretchedness" (XIV). At the time of the preparations for Caddy Jellyby's marriage "nothing belonging to the family, which it had been possible to break, was unbroken . . . ; nothing which it had been possible to spoil in any way, was unspoilt; . . . no domestic object which was capable of collecting dirt, from a dear child's knee to the door-plate, was without as much dirt as could well accumulate upon it" (XXX). The Jellyby house is perhaps the extreme case, but Skimpole's home too is "in a state of dilapidation" (XLIII), Symond's Inn, where Richard Carstone's lawyer, Vholes, lives, has been made "of old building materials, which took kindly to the dry rot and to dirt and all things decaying and dismal" (XXXIX), and Richard himself lives in a room which is full of "a great confusion of clothes, tin cases, books, boots, brushes, and portmanteaus, strewn all about the floor" (XLV). The "dusty bundles of papers" in his room seem to Esther "like dusty mirrors reflecting his own mind" (LI).

These present states of disorder are not simply inorganic formlessness; they are the terminal point of an organically interconnected series of stages which led naturally and inevitably from one to another. The present stage of rottenness is the result of an inverted process of growth, "like [that] of fungus or any unwholesome excrescence produced . . . in neglect and impurity" (XLVI). Such a process escapes from the discontinuous, but only to replace it with a mode of continuity which is apparently an irreversible growth toward death. This death will be defined as the putrefaction of every organic form and as the pulveriza-

tion of every structured inorganic thing. There is here no Spencerian
constructive law immanent in nature and guaranteeing, through the
impersonal operation of causality, the creation of ever finer and more
discriminated forms of life. Rather, it is as though the generative
cause and immanent principle of growth had been withdrawn altogether, leaving things to fall back to their primal disorder.

Sometimes this process appears, not as a certain stage which it has
now reached, but in the very midst of its happening. Although the
participles in the opening paragraphs of the novel suggested the present activity of inanimate objects, participial forms can also express the
falling away and disintegration from moment to moment of things
which are collapsing into chaos. Thus, Esther is painfully aware of
"the musty *rotting* silence of the house" where Ada and Richard are
living (LI), and in Nemo's room, "one old mat, trodden to shreds of
rope-yarn, lies *perishing* upon the hearth" (X). A description of the
beach at Deal shows it as a kind of wasteland of disunity, and ends
with the apparent metamorphosis of the inhabitants into a lower
form of existence. The heterogeneity gives way at last to a single substance into which the men seem to be transforming themselves, just as
the litter of the beach dissolves into the sea and the fog:

> The long flat beach, with its little irregular houses, wooden and brick,
> and its litter of capstans, and great boats, and sheds, and bare upright
> poles with tackle and blocks, and loose gravelly waste places overgrown
> with grass and weeds, wore as dull an appearance as any place I ever
> saw. The sea was heaving under a thick white fog; and nothing else was
> moving but a few early ropemakers, who, with the yarn twisted round
> their bodies, looked as if, tired of their present state of existence, they
> were spinning themselves into cordage. (XLV)

Perhaps the best example of this disintegration is the initial description
of Tom-all-Alone's, which makes an elaborate use of present participles to express an active process of decomposition matching the forward movement of time: "It is a street of perishing blind houses, with
their eyes stoned out; without a pane of glass, without so much as a
window-frame, with the bare blank shutters tumbling from their
hinges and falling asunder; the iron rails peeling away in flakes of rust;
the chimneys sinking in; the stone steps to every door (and every door
might be Death's Door) turning stagnant green; the very crutches on
which the ruins are propped, decaying" (VIII).

One might plot the curve of this approach to maximum entropy by a
series of crucial points. There was once evidently, long ago in the past,

a time when things were orderly, when everything fitted into its place in an organic structure, and when each individual object was itself a formal unity. From that point things passed eventually to a stage in which they were simply collections of broken objects thrown pell-mell together. Things are then like the wreckage left behind after the destruction of a civilization. Each fragmentary form once had a use and a purpose, but is now merely debris. Such collections form the contents of Krook's rag and bottle shop or of the closets of the Jellyby house:

> In all parts of the window, were quantities of dirty bottles: blacking bottles, medicine bottles, ginger-beer and soda-water bottles, pickle bottles, wine bottles, ink bottles . . . . A little way within the shop-door, lay heaps of old crackled parchment scrolls, and discoloured and dog's-eared law-papers. I could have fancied that all the rusty keys, of which there must have been hundreds huddled together as old iron, had once belonged to doors of rooms or strong chests in lawyers' offices. The litter of rags . . . might have been counsellors' bands and gowns torn up. One had only to fancy . . . that yonder bones in a corner, piled together and picked very clean, were the bones of clients, to make the picture complete. (V)

> But such wonderful things came tumbling out of the closets when they were opened—bits of mouldy pie, sour bottles, Mrs. Jellyby's caps, letters, tea, forks, odd boots and shoes of children, firewood, wafers, saucepan-lids, damp sugar in odds and ends of paper bags, footstools, blacklead brushes, bread, Mrs. Jellyby's bonnets, books with butter sticking to the binding, guttered candle-ends put out by being turned upside down in broken candlesticks, nutshells, heads and tails of shrimps, dinner-mats, gloves, coffee-grounds, umbrellas . . . . (XXX)

Not only are things moving in the direction of increasing disorder, they are also moving further and further beyond the limits of human intelligence. Whatever human meaning and order there may have been originally is now obliterated in complexity which defies comprehension: "This scarecrow of a suit has, in course of time, become so complicated, that no man alive knows what it means" (I). Even if there were some intelligible purpose in the original impetus which set the case in motion, that purpose has been utterly lost in its own self-proliferating complexity. Now the case runs automatically, without any direction from the thousands of people, suitors and lawyers, who are mere parties to it, mere instruments of its autonomous activity: "It's about a Will, and the trusts under a Will—or it was, once. It's about nothing but Costs, now. We are . . . equitably waltzing ourselves off to dusty death, about Costs. That's the great question. All the rest, by some extraordinary means, has melted away" (VIII).

But in the end even this kind of structure, a structure so elaborate that it cannot be understood by the human mind, yields to complete heterogeneity. And a world of complete heterogeneity is, paradoxically, a world of complete homogeneity. Since nothing has any relation to anything else and cannot therefore be understood in terms of a contrast to anything else, everything is, finally, the equivalent of everything else. The contents of Krook's rag and bone shop, like everything involved in Chancery, are transformed at last to mere undifferentiated dust, another form of the fog and mud which dominate the opening scene of the novel. Everything there is "wasting away and going to rack and ruin," turning into "rust and must and cobwebs" (V). The final product is made up of thousands of distinct particles, but each particle is, in the end, no more than another example of the general pulverization. So Tom-all-Alone's is at one stage of its decay like the ruined body of a man half dead and crawling with vermin: "these tumbling tenements contain, by night, a swarm of misery. As, on the ruined human wretch, vermin parasites appear, so, these ruined shelters have bred a crowd of foul existence that crawls in and out of gaps in walls and boards; and coils itself to sleep, in maggot numbers, where the rain drips in . . ." (XVI). But later on even this semblance of life disappears from the scene and Tom-all-Alone's is like the cold and lifeless moon, a "desert region unfit for life and blasted by volcanic fires" (XLVI), with a "stagnant channel of mud" for a main street (XLVI). In the end, any organic entity, whether human or material, which gets caught up in the process of decomposition becomes nothing but a powdery or pasty substance, without form or life. This process can be either a physical or a spiritual disintegration, either the destruction of the individual through his absorption in the impersonal institution of "law and equity," or the dissolution of all solid material form in "that kindred mystery, the street mud, which is made of nobody knows what, and collects about us nobody knows whence or how" (X). One of the basic symbolic equations of the novel is the suggested parallel between these two forms of disintegration.

The mud and fog of the opening paragraphs of the novel are not, we can see now, the primeval stuff out of which all highly developed forms evolve. They are the symptoms of a general return to the primal slime, a return to chaos which is going on everywhere in the novel and is already nearing its final end when the novel begins.

The human condition of the characters of *Bleak House* is, then, to be thrown into a world which is neither fresh and new nor already highly organized, but is a world which has already gone bad. From the very first moment in which they are aware of themselves at all, the characters find themselves involved in this world. Their dereliction is to be already a suitor in a case which began long before they were born, or already tainted with the quasi-sin of illegitimacy. Their mode of being in the world is to be already committed to a situation which they have not chosen.

This dereliction will never end, as long as the character is alive. It is the permanent condition of human existence in *Bleak House*. The fact that almost all of the characters in the novel are in one way or another engaged in an endless suit in Chancery is much more than a mere device of narrative unity. To be involved in an endless case, a case which can only be concluded by the total using up of both suit and suitor, becomes a symbol in the novel of what it is to be in the world at all. It is because a person is part of a process, because he is born into a case which is going on at his birth and remains unfinished throughout his life, that he cannot settle down, cannot find some definitive formulation of his identity and of his place in the world. But to be unfinished, to be open toward the future, to be evermore about to be, is, for Dickens, to be human. Richard suffers the human situation itself and defines the state of all the characters when he describes himself as living permanently in a "temporary condition" (XXIII):

"... I am a very unfortunate dog not to be more settled, but how *can* I be more settled? If you lived in an unfinished house, you couldn't settle down in it; if you were condemned to leave everything you undertook, unfinished, you would find it hard to apply yourself to anything; and yet that's my unhappy case. I was born into this unfinished contention with all its chances and changes, and it began to unsettle me before I quite knew the difference between a suit at law and a suit of clothes; and it has gone on unsettling me ever since." (XXIII)

Richard's error is not to understand that his case can never be finished, to live in the expectation of an end which will settle his life in a permanent form: "it can't last for ever. We shall come on for a final hearing, and get judgment in our favour .... These proceedings will come to a termination, and then I am provided for" (XXIII). But the nature of these proceedings is precisely to be interminable, as long as the character is alive.

For many of the characters the determining cause which has made of their situations what they irrevocably are, occurred so long before their birth that it assumes a quasi-mythical character. They attempt to trace the series of effects and causes from the present moment back retrogressively to the first cause, only to be lost in the mists and confusions of the past. Long, long ago in the past, so long ago that no one now has any direct contact with what happened then, the chain of causes and effects which has brought things to their present pass was initiated. Such characters seem to be involved in a kind of original sin for which they must innocently suffer: "How mankind ever came to be afflicted with Wiglomeration, or for whose sins these young people ever fell into a pit of it, I don't know; so it is" (VIII).

But for other characters the definitive event which has determined their lives is prior to the beginning of the novel but not prior to their birth. As in Faulkner's novels, we are presented with characters who are when we first meet them already doomed by something which happened long ago in their own lives, something which they hide carefully from the world, but on which their conscious attention is permanently fixed in a kind of retrospective fascination. All their lives are spent attempting unsuccessfully to escape from this determining moment. It is a constantly reënacted failure which only makes their lives all the more permanently attached to a past from which they cannot separate themselves, and which irrevocably defines them as what they are. The secretly obsessed quality of many of the characters in *Bleak House* makes this novel very different from *Martin Chuzzlewit*. In the earlier novel the characters either had no inner lives at all as distinct from their environments, or had subjectivities which were anonymous and empty, mere pure and vivid vision, existing only in the present. In *Bleak House,* some characters are seen as possessing, not this anonymous lucidity, but a concentrated awareness of their pasts and of their destinies. Such consciousnesses are not yet shown from the inside, as they will be in *Little Dorrit,* but their presence is unmistakably implied by the actions of the characters and revealed in occasional glimpses of their interior worlds. Of the tragedy of Boythorn's projected marriage, Jarndyce says: "That time has had its influence on all his later life" (IX, and see XLIII). And Nemo was living, we realize, in the constant suffering of the tragedy of his relations to Lady Dedlock, just as George Rouncewell's bluff exterior hides a secret remorse for having run away from home, and just as Tulkinghorn lives in a state of quiet desperation. He is shown for one moment as he is for himself, remembering a friend of his, obviously a surrogate for himself, a "man of the same mould," who "lived the same kind of life until he was seventy-five years old," and then hanged himself (XXII). But Lady Dedlock is, of course, the chief example of this theme. Her boredom hides an intense concentration on her own past, and all her attempts to cease to be the lover of Captain Hawdon only carry her more irresistibly toward her final reaffirmation of her past self. Her tragedy, like that of Racine's characters, of Hardy's, or of Faulkner's, is the tragedy of the irrevocable. Her fate is to be the doomed victim of her own past, a past which continues itself ineluctably into her present state as long as she lives.

But the determining cause which makes impotent victims of all these characters does not exist solely as a kind of mythical event occurring so long ago that no direct contact with it is possible, nor does it exist solely as an impersonal force which imposes itself from the outside on people and warps or destroys them. It may be both of these, but in its most powerful form it is immanent, present in the contemporary spiritual condition of the characters, although they may not even be consciously aware of it. It is able to get inside its victims, and inhabit them as a destructive force. It then no longer needs to exist as an exterior power, and can withdraw and disappear, leaving the possessed character to his isolated doom. Everywhere in *Bleak House* we can see the intrusion into the present of a fatally determining past from which the characters can in no way free themselves because it has become part of the very substance of their beings. In *Bleak House* the present is not really something isolated and without engagement in the past, but is the preservation of the past and its continuation in the present. Inhabited by immanent determining forces tending irreversibly toward their dissolution, the characters disintegrate, just as Grandfather Small-weed collapses "like some wound-up instrument running down" (XXXIX), and just as his daughter "dwindled away like touchwood" (XXI).

The self-enclosed life of the characters of *Bleak House* is, then, not a mechanical repetition. It is a clock that runs down, something organic which has died and decays, the entropy of an enclosed system approaching the maximum equilibrium of its forces. As in the "circumscribed universe" of Poe,[1] since there is no influx of life, energy, air, or novelty from the outside, there is a gradual exhaustion of the forces inside, a

[1] See Georges Poulet, "L'Univers circonscrit d'Edgar Poe," *Les Temps Modernes,* CXIV, CXV (1955), 2179–2204.

disaggregation of all solid forms, as all diversity is slowly transformed into a bland and motionless homogeneity. Such an enclosed system will, like a case in Chancery, eventually "die out of its own vapidity" (XXIV), or "lapse and melt away" (LXV). Beneath a carapace of solitude the will, the strength, the life of these characters exhausts itself, consumes itself in its own internal activity. So Richard, "the good consuming and consumed, the life turned sour," is slowly transformed into "the one subject that is resolving his existence into itself" (XXXIX). Wholly enclosed within his own obsession, such a character experiences a steady decomposition of his life, an acceleration toward the ultimate disorder and lifelessness of dust and mud:

> "My whole estate . . . has gone in costs. The suit, still undecided, has fallen into rack, and ruin, and despair, with everything else . . ." (XV)
>
> In the meantime [while Tom Jarndyce became absorbed in his suit], the place became dilapidated, the wind whistled through the cracked walls, the rain fell through the broken roof, the weeds choked the passage to the rotting door. (VIII)
>
> His voice had faded, with the old expression of his face, with his strength, with his anger, with his resistance to the wrongs that had at last subdued him. The faintest shadow of an object full of form and colour, is such a picture of it, as he was of the man from Shropshire whom we had spoken with before. (XXIV)
>
> . . . it is the same death eternally—inborn, inbred, engendered in the corrupted humours of the vicious body itself, and that only—Spontaneous Combustion, and none other of all the deaths that can be died. (XXXII)

Krook's death by spontaneous combustion, described in the last quotation, is of course the most notorious example of this return to homogeneity in *Bleak House*. Krook is transformed into the basic elements of the world of the novel, fog and mud. The heavy odor in the air, as if bad pork chops were frying, and the "thick yellow liquor" which forms on the window sill as Krook burns into the circumambient atmosphere, are particularly horrible versions of these elements.

But if the deterioration of the characters in *Bleak House* can appear as the inescapable fulfillment of an inner principle of corruption, it can also appear as a destiny which draws the characters from some prospective point toward their doom. Instead of being pushed from behind or from within, the characters may be attracted from the future. This may appear in the sudden collapse or dissolution of some object or person which has long been secretly mined from within by

decay, and goes to pieces in a moment when some artificial foundation
or sustaining principle gives way. So the houses in Tom-all-Alone's
collapse (XVI); so the man from Shropshire "break[s] down in an hour"
(XXIV); and so the death of Tulkinghorn seems to Lady Dedlock "but
the key-stone of a gloomy arch removed, and now the arch begins to
fall in a thousand fragments, each crushing and mangling piecemeal!"
(LV). "It was right," she says, "that all that had sustained me should
give way at once, and that I should die of terror and my conscience"
(LIX). Indeed the spontaneous combustion of Krook is just such a
rapid fulfillment of a process which has been preparing itself invisibly
for a long time, just as the stroke which paralyzes Sir Leicester makes
him physically what he spiritually has been all along, a frozen and
outmoded form of life, speaking "mere jumble and jargon" (LVI).

In all these cases, it is as though a hidden orientation suddenly
revealed itself when, all restraint gone, the character yields at last to a
destiny which has been attracting him with ever-increasing intensity.
As Bucket says, "the frost breaks up, and the water runs" (LIV). It
does not run randomly, however, but toward a center which has all
along been exerting its gravitational pull. This pull does not now
commence, but only now manifests itself. And so Miss Flite can speak
of the Court of Chancery not as a first cause, but as a final cause drawing men to their ruin by means of its irresistible magnetic attraction:

> "There's a cruel attraction in the place. You *can't* leave it. And you
> *must* expect. . . . It's the Mace and Seal upon the table."
> What could they do, did she think? I mildly asked her.
> "Draw," returned Miss Flite. "Draw people on, my dear. Draw peace
> out of them. Sense out of them. Good looks out of them. Good qualities
> out of them. I have felt them even drawing my rest away in the night.
> Cold and glittering devils!" (XXXV)

For many characters their disintegration is not so much the working
out of a chain of causes and effects begun long in the past as it is the
fatal convergence of their inner lives and their external situations
toward a point where both will coincide at their death. Richard had
mistakenly believed that "either the suit must be ended, . . . or the
suitor" (LI). But he is slowly consumed by his vampire-like lawyer,
Vholes, just as the case of Jarndyce and Jarndyce is entirely consumed
in costs. When both processes are finally complete, Vholes gives "one
gasp as if he had swallowed the last morsel of his client" (LXV). The
termination of the interminable case coincides necessarily with the

exhaustion of all the money involved in it, and with the simultaneous death of Richard. All of these events inevitably occur together as the vanishing point toward which all the parallel motions have been converging, as toward their final cause. This temporal progression is glimpsed by Esther in a momentary scene which prognosticates Richard's fate. It is a good example of the way scenes in Dickens which are initially merely narrative realism are transformed into symbolic expressions of the entire destiny of a character:

> "I shall never forget those two seated side by side in the lantern's light; Richard, all flush and fire and laughter, with the reins in his hand; Mr. Vholes, quite still, black-gloved, and buttoned up, looking at him as if he were looking at his prey and charming it. I have before me the whole picture of the warm dark night, the summer lightning, the dusty track of road closed in by hedgerows and high trees, the gaunt pale horse with his ears pricked up, and the driving away at speed to Jarndyce and Jarndyce." (XXXVII)

In the same way the life and death of Jo the crossing sweeper are made symbolic. During his life Jo has been continually forced to "move on." His death is imaged as the "breaking down" of a cart that as it disintegrates approaches closer and closer to an end point which will be its total fragmentation: "For the cart so hard to draw, is near its journey's end, and drags over stony ground. All round the clock it labours up the broken steps, shattered and worn. Not many times can the sun rise, and behold it still upon its weary road" (XLVII). And so the death of Lady Dedlock is described as a journey which is the slow closing in of her destiny: "When I saw my Lady yesterday, . . . she looked to me . . . as if the step on the Ghost's Walk had almost walked her down" (LVIII). Like Richard's future, the prospect before and beside the road which she is journeying is getting narrower and narrower. The end point will be her death, the complete extinction of all possibility of choice or movement: "The dark road I have trodden for so many years will end where it will. I follow it alone to the end, whatever the end be. . . . [Danger] has closed around me, almost as awfully as if these woods of Chesney Wold had closed around the house; but my course through it is the same" (XXXVI).

But this sudden break-up of things when the keystone of the arch has been removed may be imaged not as a narrowing, but as a descent deeper and deeper into the pit of the dark and unformed. When the fragile foundations which have been precariously upholding things give way, there is a sudden drop vertically into infernal depths. The

Chancery suit is a "dead sea" (XXXVII), and Richard "sink[s] deeper and deeper into difficulty every day, continually hoping and continually disappointed, conscious of change upon change for the worse in [himself]" (XXXIX). Mr. Snagsby, being led by Bucket and his colleagues into the heart of Tom-all-Alone's, "feels as if he were going, every moment deeper and deeper down, into the infernal gulf" (XXII). What he sees is like a vision of hell itself. Not the least horrible part of this visionary experience is the way the human dwellers in Tom-all-Alone's seem to have been transformed into the elements they live in, the fog and mud:

> . . . Mr. Snagsby passes along the middle of a villainous street, undrained, unventilated, deep in black mud and corrupt water . . . . [T]he crowd flows round, and from its squalid depths obsequious advice heaves up to Mr. Bucket. Whenever they move, and the angry bull's-eyes glare, it fades away, and flits about them up the alleys, and in the ruins, and behind the walls . . . . (XXII)

But it is Lady Dedlock's journey to death, after the murder of Tulkinghorn has revealed her secret, which is the most elaborate dramatization of this kind of disintegration. The chase after Lady Dedlock by Bucket and Esther is not simply a Victorian melodrama. It is a subtly symbolic dramatization of the destiny of Lady Dedlock and of her relation to her daughter. Once her "freezing mood" is melted, she rapidly becomes, like Poe's mesmerized man when his trance is broken, what she has really been all along: dead. The thawing snow, the change of direction from a centrifugal flight outward from the city to a return to the center of disintegration and corruption where her dead lover lies buried, her disguise in the dress of a brickmaker's wife whose baby has died, all these function symbolically. Here, more intensely than for any other character, we experience the descent into formlessness which follows inevitably the failure to achieve a proper relation to the onward motion of time.

Bucket's chase after Lady Dedlock is presented through Esther's eyes. All that happens has for her a visionary, dreamlike quality: "I was far from sure that I was not in a dream" (LVII); ". . . the stained house fronts put on human shapes and looked at me; . . . great water-gates seemed to be opening and closing in my head, or in the air; . . . the unreal things were more substantial than the real" (LIX). The dominant symbol of the whole sequence is contained here in the image of water-gates opening and closing. The process of Lady Dedlock's dying after her freezing mood has broken is mirrored in nature itself in the melting snow which lies everywhere that night: "From the portico, from the eaves, from the parapet, from every ledge and post and pillar, drips the thawed snow. It has crept, as if for shelter, into the lintels of the great door—under it, into the corners of the windows, into every chink and crevice of retreat, and there wastes and dies" (LVIII).

At the center of all this melting is perhaps the river, which is reached by a "labyrinth of streets" (LVII). There, Bucket fears, Lady Dedlock may be found: ". . . he gazed into the profound black pit of water, with a face that made my heart die within me. The river had a fearful look, so overcast and secret, creeping away so fast between the low flat lines of shore: so heavy with indistinct and awful shapes, both of substance and shadow: so deathlike and mysterious" (LVII). But the real center, reached by "descending into a deeper complication of such streets" (LIX), is the pauper graveyard, the low point into which all things are resolving, the center of anonymity, putrefaction, and formlessness, the point at which Lady Dedlock at last becomes herself at the very moment of her death:

> The gate was closed. Beyond it, was a burial-ground—a dreadful spot in which the night was very slowly stirring; but where I could dimly see heaps of dishonoured graves and stones, hemmed in by filthy houses, with a few dull lights in their windows, and on whose walls a thick humidity broke out like a disease. On the step at the gate, drenched in the fearful wet of such a place, which oozed and splashed down everywhere, I saw, with a cry of pity and horror, a woman lying—Jenny, the mother of the dead child. (LIX)

But the woman is, of course, really Lady Dedlock, herself the mother of a dead child, the child Esther might have been. That Lady Dedlock's death is in a way a liberation is suggested by her contrary movements during her flight out from the city and then back toward its dark center. At the extremity of her outward flight she sends her surrogate, the brickmaker's wife, on out into the open country to lead her pursuers astray. This woman, in her movement toward freedom and openness, is Lady Dedlock's representative only because Lady Dedlock herself voluntarily chooses to return to her destined death at Nemo's grave, or, rather, to her death at a place where she is still shut off by one final symbolic barrier, the closed gate, from union with her dead lover. In assuming at last the self she has been fleeing for so long, Lady Dedlock achieves the only kind of freedom possible in Dickens' world, the freedom to be one's destined self, the Kierkegaardian freedom to will to accept oneself as what one already irrevocably is.

But for most of the characters, even such a narrow freedom is not possible. Their decomposition happens to them, rather than being chosen, and the image for their final end is not even permitted the hint of life-giving regeneration suggested by Lady Dedlock's melting from her frozen state. Their lives are single cases of a vast process of disintegration into dust, and the entire world of the novel is being transformed into "ashes . . . falling on ashes, and dust on dust" (XXXIX):

> In his lowering magazine of dust, the universal article into which his papers and himself, and all his clients, and all things of earth, animate and inanimate, are resolving, Mr. Tulkinghorn sits at one of the open windows . . . . (XXII)

From *The Dickens Theatre*

by *Robert E. Garis*

Dickens's attack on System consists for the most part of a gallery of exhibits of human behaviour. He constructs this gallery by a remarkable capitalization on his early methods of characterization. In the Dickens theatre we are always an audience for the people, the landscapes, the houses, we meet; in *Bleak House* Dickens has made us into a special kind of audience, one that instantly tries to see what relationship each new person, each new house, each new landscape, has to the great case against System. And no one has any trouble seeing these relationships. Mrs. Jellyby, for instance, is the overlord of a tiny system of organized benevolence, whom Mr. Jarndyce sent Esther, Ada, and Richard to visit "on purpose"—he says so explicitly (VI). What did they learn, and how did they learn it? Not a moment is lost in answering these questions: not a detail connected with the name Jellyby but serves as a piece of evidence for Dickens's, and in this case also Mr. Jarndyce's, attack on System. The Jellybys live "in a narrow street of high houses, like an oblong cistern to hold the fog. There was a confused little crowd of people, principally children, gathered about the house at which we stopped, which had a tarnished brass plate on the door, with the inscription, JELLYBY" (IV). Every detail here is a judgement, and the judgement is emphatic and simple. The narrowness of the street speaks instantly of a lack of freedom, and attacks that condition. A street should not be a cistern to hold the fog, and if Mrs. Jellyby chooses to live on this street it means that she likes fog. In the first chapter we saw the Lord High Chancellor sitting at the centre of the fog; Mrs. Jellyby is then like him. Crowds of people should not be confused, children should not be in crowds, a brass plate should not be tarnished. Because we are in the Dickens theatre, listening to Dickens's

From The Dickens Theatre *by Robert E. Garis (Oxford: The Clarendon Press, 1965), pp. 109–24. Copyright © 1965 by the Clarendon Press. Reprinted by permission of the publisher.*

attack on System, we translate every detail into a judgement with a rapidity which makes the judgements very simple ones.

The sense of confusion, constriction, and neglect is brought to an immediate focus by the fact that the little crowd is watching Peepy Jellyby, who has caught his head in the area railings. The various responses to Peepy's predicament are also immediately translated into judgements. Esther is sympathetic, but Mr. Guppy tells her that this sort of occurrence is too commonplace to be worried about: she is advised to be careful about herself. The milkman and the beadle are inefficiently trying to extricate Peepy: they are well-intentioned but caring for little children is not their "natural" role. Esther is a natural young woman; natural women know how to take care of children; Esther suggests the proper method of releasing Peepy and it works.

When Esther finds out that, contrary to her deduction, Peepy's mother is not at home, the little scene is complete and its emblematic nature clear. The child is in trouble because it is being tended by the wrong people, by servants, milkmen, beadles, instead of by its mother. Mothers can keep their children's heads out of area railings, and this is their natural function. When natural functions are working naturally, all goes well. When not, the result is dirt, confusion, loss of freedom, the well-intentioned (or ill-intentioned) interference of incompetent public servants or of System itself.

The rest of this first glimpse of the Jellybys amplifies the disorder and also focuses the explanation for it more exactly. Mrs. Jellyby has displaced her attention from the correct objects of her responsibility, her children and her husband and her housekeeping, to the operation of a system of benevolence, an abstract, distorted, impersonal substitute for her natural instinct to take care of people. She loses contact not only with her children but with all human individuals, and thinks only in terms of numbers and groups: "We hope by this time next year to have from a hundred and fifty to two hundred healthy families cultivating coffee and educating the natives of Borrioboola-Gha, on the left bank of the Niger" (IV). The only single human beings she really notices are those like herself, similarly dehumanized, whose sole emotion is anxiety "for the welfare of their species all over the country." These people she calls "private individuals" to distinguish them from "public bodies" (IV).

The relationship between Mrs. Jellyby and Chancery is clear: both are initially motivated by a genuine human interest—benevolence and justice respectively—but both have lost sight of the single human being and are concerned with the operation of a System. And the actual workings of both systems concern, not even "public bodies" and "plaintiffs," but material objects, paraphernalia. In Chancery, the "maces, or petty-bags, or privy-purses" (I) deal mainly with "bills, cross-bills, answers, rejoinders, injunctions, affidavits, issues, references to masters, masters' reports, mountains of costly nonsense" (I). These are parodied in the contents of Krook's warehouse: "quantities of dirty bottles: blacking bottles, medicine bottles, ginger-beer and soda-water bottles, pickle bottles, wine bottles, ink bottles . . . heaps of old crackled parchment scrolls, and discoloured and dog's-eared law-papers . . . rusty keys, of which there must have been hundreds huddled together as old iron" (V). In both instances, the tools for the furthering of human interests are prized in themselves, not for what they can do for human beings. Krook merely collects these tools: "Everything seemed to be bought, and nothing to be sold there" (V). Chancery is more foolish and more dangerous because it seems to carry on a kind of action with the tools, but the tools make contact only with other tools—bills speak only to cross-bills, references to masters are answered by masters' reports. In Mrs. Jellyby's system, even the two hundred healthy families on the left bank of the Niger are shadowy and unreal in comparison with the actual paraphernalia of Mrs. Jellyby's enormous "correspondence," the "litter" of papers with which her room, and her life, is entirely filled. "Correspondence" ought to represent clarity of communication between single human beings but figures instead as litter and dirt. The ink with which this correspondence is written only dirties Caddy Jellyby. But although Caddy Jellyby looks discontented and sulky, Mrs. Jellyby is not aware that she is deep in dirt, but sits "serene" in her system, as the Lord High Chancellor sits "with a foggy glory round his head, softly fenced in with crimson cloth and curtains" (I).

The Law is more dangerous than Mrs. Jellyby's system. Mr. Gridley "can by no means be made to understand that the Chancellor is legally ignorant of his existence after making it desolate for a quarter of a century" (I), and the Lord High Chancellor has simply forgotten, softly fenced in with crimson cloth and curtains as he is, that the chief party in the court's favourite comic case, Jarndyce and Jarndyce, has committed suicide. He has to be reminded of this fact in the foggy talk that passes for human communication in Chancery: "Begludship's pardon—victim of rash action—brains" (I). But although Mrs. Jellyby thinks her children are "naughty" when they only want a little attention, nevertheless the children do exist and they do call themselves to her attention. (Mr. Jellyby, however, has been reduced to a cipher.) Caddy Jellyby, indeed, emerges from the litter and dirt to a more natural life—we will examine her more carefully later. There is something perhaps even positive in the fact that part of the "litter" in Mrs. Jellyby's household is actual dirt. This system has not been perfected to its ultimate inhumanity: the sinister interaction of one tool with another. There is no dirt, one fancies, in Mrs. Pardiggle's household, and the five little Pardiggles are already, although unwillingly, engaged in the charitable distribution of their allowances. The Smallweed family and the Vholes family are horrid parodies of family life, guaranteeing the sterility of the household instead of contradicting it. There are only adult children in the Smallweed house, genuine childishness arriving only in the form of senility. And Mr. Vholes's remarkable statement, "I both have, and am, a father" (XXXIX), is pure process: the systematic exactness of the syntax takes all hope of living human impulse out of these family relations, reducing the elements of the sentence, and the sexual act, to the correctly functioning parts of a machine. But there is some hope of life in Mrs. Jellyby's system.

Mrs. Jellyby, once presented, never changes. When she reappears from time to time, she is engaged as always in her correspondence, serene, untidy, mildly displeased with her naughty children, but tolerant of their unilluminated state. We never learn anything new about her; she fits E. M. Forster's category of "flat" characters perfectly in that she reappears entire, with all her clothes, her gestures, her speech, intact. She does not change, she does not grow, she never engages in any dramatic action, she has no centre of self and therefore we do not engage with her. When she reappears there is little pretence of verisimilitude in Dickens's bringing her back: Esther is sent to visit her again "on purpose," though this time it is Dickens's, not Mr. Jarndyce's purpose: to give the audience a repeat performance of an interesting and amusing and instructive theatrical routine. And in this respect she is quite like Dickens's earlier characters.

But there is one significant difference between Dickens's methods in *Bleak House* and his methods earlier. Since every detail about Mrs. Jellyby is now meaningful in moral, judgmental terms, every characterization is offered to us for immediate judgement and condemnation, and therefore her lack of inner life, her inability to change, her inability to engage in any action is also offered to us for condemnation. When Caddy Jellyby tells her that she is going to be married, Mrs. Jellyby is offered an opportunity to engage in a human action; the fact that she does not take the opportunity is the final confirmation of her systematized existence, her inability to meet experience, and this inability is very firmly brought to our attention and condemned.

The majority of the characters in *Bleak House,* who make up the majority of the exhibits in the great case against System, are, like Mrs. Jellyby, systematized. Whether they are rulers or victims, Dickens makes us see that they never change, that they are not truly alive, that they are subordinated entirely to routine. Dickens views these systematized people with varying degrees of condemnation, with horror in some cases, with amused tolerance in others. Taken together, they very richly embody a powerful demonstration and denunciation of the world of System.

This world, the "world of *Bleak House,*" is not a world we live in —more accurately, not a world we have the illusion of living in, as we have the illusion of living in the world of novels as diverse in method and tone as *Emma* or *The Trial* or *Resurrection* or *The Sound and the Fury.* The world of *Bleak House* is a theatrical performance rendered by a theatrical artist who is proving a case. Accordingly, the standards by which we judge it are those by which we judge an argument: we do not ask, then, "Is it real?" but "Is it convincing?"

The sheer number of the systematized beings in *Bleak House* is large enough to give a convincing sense that a whole world is being examined; and their variety is a convincing representation of the variety we expect to encounter in the world. There are, for instance, the several representatives of the system of Law: Mr. Tulkinghorn, Conversation Kenge, Mr. Guppy, Mr. Vholes; and then several others who either serve or parody the Law: Mr. Krook, Mr. Snagsby, Coavinses, the Smallweeds. The number of these is large enough to make the insidious power of the Law believable. And the differences between them and our different responses to them are vivid and pointed enough to make the case seem a fair one: we seem to have looked at all sides of the argument. This is true of all the other systems in the book.

Granted this quantity and variety of the dehumanized beings, no organic and progressive interaction between them will be necessary to show this world in action. These mechanical people are by definition incapable of knowing each other as individuals, of engaging with each other's minds, even of adapting their behaviour to each other. Some recognitions take place: Mrs. Pardiggle honours Mrs. Jellyby (though she criticizes her too), the Law respects Philanthropy and Fashion and is respected by them in turn, Mr. Skimpole conspires with Mr. Vholes.

And the victims reach out ineffectually to each other: Mr. Snagsby to Jo and Guster, the brickmakers' wives to Jo, Jo to Nemo, Caddy to her father. But these poignant gestures are always furtive and guilty, and they are as nearly mute as articulate human behaviour can be. Indeed, since the instruments of articulate human behaviour have all been thoroughly systematized, these little moments of communication between victims of the System are close to being merely instinctive, and it is as such that Dickens approves of them. In opposition to all this, most of the articulate conversations we hear in *Bleak House* manifest a decided lack of communication.

The System in action, then, comes to us for the most part as a richly varied series of encounters between people who cannot talk with each other and who therefore can only perform their own natures in antiphonal duet with each other. Dickens has invented a remarkable number of these duets and there is a remarkable variety in them. For only one instance, consider the meeting between Mr. Skimpole and Coavinses early in the novel, an encounter between an apparent victim who is really a parasitic ruler of the System and an official representative of the System who is really a pathetic victim. The failure to communicate is complete, but as we watch this encounter we sense that we are watching evidence for a case which is being very richly and subtly argued, with plenty of attention to the exceptions. Or consider the entire "life" of Snagsby. Mr. Snagsby's manner never changes: apologetic and loyal subservience to System linked with furtive, embarrassed benevolence, his periphrastic language filled with the deference towards his overlords he knows he is expected to feel and which he almost entirely does feel, though he cannot understand why things do not work out for happiness when he obeys all the rules. We see him first in his own proper, local, and domestic slavery to Mrs. Snagsby. Then in his professional slavery to Mr. Tulkinghorn. Then in half-hearted, unintentionally rebellious subservience to Mr. Chadband, then skilfully bullied into silence by the ambiguous Bucket. We see him with beadles and policemen, with Guster and Mr. Guppy, with Mademoiselle Hortense, with Allan Woodcourt, finally with Esther. Always he is the same and we never learn anything more about him than we found out at his first introduction; but the number and the variety of situations in which he appears keep him interesting.

In the last analysis what makes this curious kind of action believable, as the action of a believable world, is that such writing calls for a gift which Dickens possessed in abundance. We never tire of unchanging, undeveloping, unacting Mr. Snagsby because of the inexhaustible inventiveness with which Dickens reimpersonates his original conception whenever the occasion asks him to. This is perhaps Dickens's most important single creative talent; certainly it is a talent without which the copiousness of his theatrical art would be impossible. But it is a beautiful and valuable talent, as well as a practical one. For it makes it possible for Dickens to enact, in his own performances in his own theatre, exactly the fundamental energy and generosity of instinctual life from which his attack on System derives. I cannot quote an adequate example of Dickens's amazing inventiveness in this respect, since the whole point is that this invention carries him successfully through every single appearance of Snagsby. But here is one important element of the impersonation of Mr. Snagsby in its first appearance and in a repeat performance:

> But these vague whisperings may arise from Mr. Snagsby's being, in his way, rather a meditative and poetical man; loving to walk in Staple Inn in the summer time, and to observe how countrified the sparrows and the leaves are; also to lounge about the Rolls Yard of a Sunday afternoon, and to remark (if in good spirits) that there were old times once, and that you'd find a stone coffin or two, now, under that chapel, he'll be bound, if you was to dig for it. He solaces his imagination, too, by thinking of the many Chancellors and Vices, and Masters of the Rolls, who are deceased; and he gets such a flavour of the country out of telling the two 'prentices how he *has* heard say that a brook 'as clear as crystial' once ran right down the middle of Holborn, when Turnstile really was a turnstile, leading slap away into the meadows—gets such a flavour of the country out of this, that he never wants to go there. (X)
>
> He has more leisure for musing in Staple Inn and in the Rolls Yard, during the long vacation, than at other seasons; and he says to the two 'prentices, what a thing it is in such hot weather to think that you live in an island, with the sea a-rolling and a-bowling right round you. (XIX)

The repeat performance adds nothing new to our understanding of Snagsby; the remarkable thing is how exactly it says what the earlier example said, and yet how delicately particularized an image of Snagsby is rendered by both examples. Mr. Snagsby is dreaming of freedom, and the dream is pathetically timid, touchingly undemanding of life. The point is made so affectionately and with such precision in the image of the lost Holborn spring that it would seem all but impossible for Dickens to say the same thing with different material without producing a merely mechanical variation. But the repeat performance is even more poignant than the first.

Dickens's image of the world of System depends on this basic talent of his theatrical art not only for its argumentative success but for its moral beauty and value. I have spoken often of Dickens's overt purposes in *Bleak House* as argumentative, and so they are, very loudly and insistently so. The question arises, and not only for the oversensitive modern mind, whether there is not something rather unlovely in the contrived rhetoric of this loud, insistent, vehement voice which is so eager to denounce what it hates and to convince us by this denunciation. If we sense purposeful contrivances and manipulations on every page of *Bleak House,* what prevents us from getting an overpowering, overriding impression of the human will in action? Why do these loud points and purposes not come to seem an imposition on us, a tyranny over us which is at least as oppressive as the tyranny of Chancery?

For contrivance is surely observable in the two passages about Mr. Snagsby which I have quoted. The theatrical artist is clearly enough working to plan here too, the plan being to reimpersonate one of his own exhibits. It is just as clear that he proceeds with the most knowing consciousness of what his plan requires of him; he has to make up another image of Snagsby's timid dream of freedom. The simple fact is that he can really do this; the central and wonderful truth about Dickens, which silences our criticism, is that he can perform his own plan with a spontaneous energy of invention which entirely burns away the atmosphere of mechanically insensitive wilfulness. The planning remains perfectly obvious, but there is new life available to the artist at every moment as he performs his plans. Dickens's theatrical impersonation of the world of System is as alive as its subject is dead. And, in the Dickens theatre, this means that we believe he is telling the truth.

What the world of System lacks, of course, is the complexity that goes with drama. It is as flat as its inhabitants, and this is inevitable and right. A mechanical being cannot embody any very complex meaning and cannot be the vehicle for any very complex judgement. Mrs. Jellyby, Mr. Snagsby, and the rest of the mechanized characters are assessed with accuracy and often with subtlety, and with a great range of feeling and tone. Dickens has clearly demonstrated why we cannot take these characters seriously as morally active human beings with inner lives. But this means that the moral judgements embodied by these characters and their world are not complex moral judgements.

Dickens's attitude towards this world is a serious one, in the sense that it is impassioned and urgent and compelling. But his judgement is that it cannot for a moment be accepted as a possible way of life for human beings. It is a mistake from first to last for human beings to enter into System, for System is absolutely hostile to everything that makes them human. System, then, is not *criticized* as a complex moral phenomenon, but single-mindedly denounced and rejected.

In describing this actionless world of System, I have, as the reader will have realized, ignored some important elements in *Bleak House*. There are, in fact, some actions in the novel which yield a more complex view of human nature than the simple denunciation of System. Caddy Jellyby marries Prince Turveydrop; Rosa, Lady Dedlock's maid, marries Watt Rouncewell; Richard Carstone marries Ada; Esther marries Allan Woodcourt—here are four images of the free continuing of human life. How does System make room for them? Dickens also organizes and gives forward movement to much of the novel by focusing on Lady Dedlock's guilty secret and the various mysterious investigations of it, both comic and sinister, which occupy so many of the characters in this world of System. What does this whole process tell us about System?

Caddy Jellyby's act of life is one of Dickens's triumphs of invention and of tone. Mrs. Jellyby introduces Caddy to her visitors as "my eldest daughter, who is my amanuensis," and the solemn systematic word contrasts pointedly with the actual girl:

> But what principally struck us was a jaded, and unhealthy-looking, though by no means plain girl, at the writing-table, who sat biting the feather of her pen, and staring at us. I suppose nobody ever was in such a state of ink. And, from her tumbled hair to her pretty feet, which were disfigured with frayed and broken satin slippers trodden down at heel, she really seemed to have no article of dress upon her, from a pin upwards, that was in its proper condition or its right place. (IV)

When Caddy comes sulkily to Esther's room the same night she has come for help towards being a natural young woman. She looks enviously at the sleeping Ada: "But knows a quantity, I suppose? Can dance, and play music, and sing? She can talk French, I suppose, and do geography, and globes, and needlework, and everything?" (IV). This is the neglected and deprived girl's fantasy image of natural womanliness: what Esther teaches Caddy is plain sewing. But Caddy has pretty feet and wears satin slippers, and her own independent motion towards natural life takes the form of going to dancing school. This is fully meaningful—Esther does not scold her for it—because the Jellyby children have not been allowed to play without being called naughty by their mother, and because Caddy in fact ends up working at dancing. This progress is viewed with a delicate and perfectly controlled irony by Dickens. Caddy really succeeds only in entering yet another system, that of organized grace and "deportment," and her new master, old Mr. Turveydrop, is a more demanding one than Mrs. Jellyby. Yet in this odd profession she does work which seems to us real and good, because it is motivated by love for her little husband with a dog's name, Prince Turveydrop (who was actually named after the Prince Regent). Caddy herself expresses a half-aware ironic view of the conditions of her life which comes close to real insight. Here is her first account of the little dancing-apprentices:

> The notion of the apprentices was still so odd to me, that I asked Caddy if there were many of them?
> "Four," said Caddy. "One in-door, and three out. They are very good children; only when they get together they *will* play—children-like—instead of attending to their work. So the little boy you saw just now waltzes by himself in the empty kitchen, and we distribute the others over the house as well as we can." (XXXVIII)

This sounds just enough like Mrs. Jellyby's view of children to show that Caddy is still implicated in System, but the point is charmingly made and Caddy is affectionate towards the children and annoyed with them only because she wants to do her own job well. And then there is a clearer realization: "when I put up the window, and see them standing on the door-step with their little pumps under their arms, I am actually reminded of the Sweeps." (XXXVIII) Here Caddy get the funny pathos about the dancing-apprentices across to the reader and to herself.

Caddy's womanly instincts are purely maternal, towards Peepy, towards her father, and towards her husband, whom she calls her darling child:

> I curtseyed to a little blue-eyed fair man of youthful appearance, with flaxen hair parted in the middle, and curling at the ends all round his head. He had a little fiddle, which we used to call at school a kit, under his left arm, and its little bow in the same hand. His little dancing shoes were particularly diminutive, and he had a little innocent, feminine manner, which not only appealed to me in an amiable way, but made

this singular effect upon me: that I received the impression that he was
like his mother, and that his mother had not been much considered or
well used. (XIV)

The child of this marriage is rather pointedly symbolic, but Dickens's
delicacy of touch carries the day:

> such a tiny old-faced mite, with a countenance that seemed to be scarcely
> anything but cap-border, and a little lean, long-fingered hand, always
> clenched under its chin. It would lie in this attitude all day, with its
> bright specks of eyes open, wondering (as I used to imagine) how it came
> to be so small and weak. Whenever it was moved it cried; but at all other
> times it was so patient, that the sole desire of its life appeared to be,
> to lie quiet, and think. It had curious little dark veins in its face, and
> curious little dark marks under its eyes, like faint remembrances of poor
> Caddy's inky days; and altogether, to those who were not used to it, it
> was quite a piteous little sight. (L)

The theatricality of Dickens's art makes it possible for us to consent to
"read" the meaning of this symbolic child (who turns out to be deaf
and dumb) as straightforwardly and simply as it was invented. Herein
lies the advantage of Dickens's obvious rhetorical intentions. For in
non-theatrical, non-rhetorical fiction, where there is a consistent dramatic pressure within the scene, we could not contemplate a symbolic
figure like this one with anything like the mild pathos which is possible
in the Dickens theatre. Consider our feelings about Benjy in Faulkner's
The Sound and the Fury, who is surely as meaningful—and as inten-
tional—a symbol of bad blood as Caddy's baby. We are not, for
Benjy, the sympathetic and pitying audience that we are for the pa-
tient hopelessness of Dickens's symbolic figure. With Benjy, we are
engaged in a dramatic situation, we participate in the intensities of
feeling directly, we *live with him* in an illusion of reality. And, in fact,
we watch Benjy dribble and drool and weep, nor are we insulated from
disgust by anything like Dickens's theatrical presence, performing these
painful things before us. Accordingly, we experience a painfully (and
beautifully) intense *complexity* of attitude towards Benjy, which in
turn is the necessary preparation for our intense feeling of admiration
and love for Dilsey.

If we were similarly engaged in a dramatic scene when we encounter
Caddy's husband and her baby, we would experience a feeling of horror
at the distortion and emotional poverty of Caddy's new life. There is
no horror engendered by Dickens's performance of his exhibit and

Dickens knows how to arouse horror when he wants to, though, of course, again a theatrical horror. It is pathos Dickens is after in the present instance, and that is what he achieves. The fact that it is a rather comfortable and easy pathos is a necessary result of Dickens's theatrical art and its conditions; we are in the extremely public intimacy of a theatre, we are not in an illusion of reality, we are not being led to experience imaginatively what Caddy's life is really like. We are in contact with the voice of a theatrical performer, obedient to that voice, assured by that voice. And we feel ourselves to have been watching a very touchingly sad and delicate exhibition of the limitations of life within System.

What is true of Caddy's baby is true of all the symbolic figures in *Bleak House,* and indeed in all of Dickens's work with the exception of *Great Expectations.* I am an enthusiastic admirer of Dickens's symbolic methods: he is usually in complete control of them and brilliantly inventive in performing them. But his symbols are part of his theatrical mode, and they function quite differently from symbols in non-theatrical art. In non-theatrical art a symbol is valuable because it can be implicated in a complex dramatic action and can therefore serve as the focus for a complex of attitudes towards a theme of which the symbol is also the objectification. Moreover, because the theme is thus genuinely objectified and genuinely implicated in a dramatic action, the attitudes towards it can be expressed with the unparaphrasable subtlety and precision, above all with the ambiguity, which non-symbolic art cannot achieve except by discursive analysis. A conveniently obvious instance is the cherry orchard in Chekhov's play, which expresses the rich complexity and ambiguity of Chekhov's attitude towards the passing of an old order. As the various characters discuss the cherry orchard, argue about it, make decisions about it and act on them, contemplate it, or even ignore it, all these attitudes towards the old order come together in a rich and living unity which would be difficult to achieve without the use of symbolic methods. We become engaged with all the characters in the play, we have the illusion of living with them, and they in turn are engaged with the symbolic object, they live with it; and in this way the object itself comes to be extraordinarily resonant, subtly and complexly expressive.

Except in *Great Expectations,* this never happens in Dickens's use of symbols. Mrs. Jellyby is a symbolic figure, but we do not live with her. We observe her as an exhibit. What she means is vividly embodied, but it is very simple too, and our attitude towards her is correspond-ingly simple. This is true of the fog in London, the rain in Lincoln-shire, of all the landscapes and houses and rooms—each one symbolic —in which the people in the novel are exhibited to us. None of these symbols is the vehicle for complex meaning like Chekhov's cherry orchard. Consider the description of Bleak House itself:

It was one of those delightfully irregular houses where you go up and down steps out of one room into another, and where you come upon more rooms when you think you have seen all there are, and where there is a bountiful provision of little halls and passages, and where you find still older cottage-rooms in unexpected places, with lattice windows and green growth pressing through them. Mine, which we entered first, was of this kind, with an up-and-down roof, that had more corners in it than I ever counted afterwards, and a chimney (there was a wood-fire on the hearth) paved all around with pure white tiles, in every one of which a bright miniature of the fire was blazing. Out of this room, you went down two steps, into a charming little sitting-room, looking down upon a flower-garden, which room was henceforth to belong to Ada and me. Out of this you went up three steps, into Ada's bed-room, which had a fine broad window, commanding a beautiful view (we saw a great ex-panse of darkness lying underneath the stars), to which there was a hollow window-seat, in which, with a spring-lock, three dear Adas might have been lost at once. Out of this room, you passed into a little gallery, with which the other best rooms (only two) communicated, and so, by a little staircase of shallow steps, with a number of corner stairs in it, con-sidering its length, down into the hall. But if, instead of going out at Ada's door, you came back into my room, and went out at the door by which you had entered it, and turned up a few crooked steps that branched off in an unexpected manner from the stairs, you lost yourself in passages, with mangles in them, and three-cornered tables, and a Native-Hindoo chair, which was also a sofa, a box, and a bedstead, and looked in every form something between a bamboo skeleton and a great bird-cage, and had been brought from India nobody knew by whom or when. From these, you came on Richard's room, which was part library, part sitting-room, part bed-room, and seemed indeed a comfortable com-pound of many rooms. Out of that, you went straight, with a little interval of passage, to the plain room where Mr. Jarndyce slept, all the year round, with his window open, his bedstead without any furniture standing in the middle of the floor for more air, and his cold-bath gaping for him in a smaller room adjoining. Out of that, you came into another passage, where there were back-stairs, and where you could hear the horses being rubbed down, outside the stable, and being told to Hold up and Get over, as they slipped about very much on the uneven stones.

Or you might, if you came out at another door (every room had at least two doors), go straight down to the hall again by half-a-dozen steps and a low archway, wondering how you got back there, or had ever got out of it. (VI)

This house is obviously a symbol: one immediately proceeds to inter-preting it. But it does not speak for itself: we are conscious that the theatrical artist is speaking his purposes through the symbol. (This consciousness is buttressed by the fact that Mr. Jarndyce is also show-ing his house to the young people "for a purpose.") The artist has sev-eral purposes in mind, not exactly contradictory but definitely differ-ent ones, and his procedure is simply to add another room for each purpose. Dickens wants the house to speak about Mr. Jarndyce's kind solicitude for Esther and Ada, so he makes it the kind of house which these two young girls can find charming and delightful. Because Mr. Jarndyce himself is charmingly and delightfully eccentric, the quaint-ness of Bleak House is not altogether inappropriate for him. But it is somewhat inappropriate: it is too feminine, too much of a cosy retreat, for a man with supposedly serious moral purposes and an active phil-anthropic life. A special room, expressive of manly freedom and seri-ous activity, is accordingly added for Mr. Jarndyce. Mr. Jarndyce is hopeful that Richard will settle down to serious work too, but he is still only a boy: Dickens contrives a suitable room for him too. It is clear that Dickens wants the whole house to be expressive of the domes-tic virtues and at the same time of freedom and life within the domestic virtues, for Mr. Jarndyce builds an exact replica of Bleak House for Esther and Allan Woodcourt. The house does serve well enough for this purpose, though its feminine charm somewhat gets in the way. The symbol achieves what it sets out to achieve and the reader gets the point throughout.

PART TWO

View Points

William York Tindall: From *The Literary Symbol*

When we read a symbolist novel for the first time or even the second or third, we may find it slight or even naturalistic. When we read it again, however, we find that the concrete particulars and arrangement which gave us that impression are there to carry meanings beyond immediate significance; and as we proceed, a greater meaning gradually emerges. Each rereading adds fresh discoveries, changing our idea of the whole until we despair of reaching the end of that suggestive complexity. Reading in groups—where each member, stimulated by the others and rebuking their occasional irrelevance or excess, contributes his understanding of the text—seems the best approach. Still, of such works the last word will not be spoken, for since the effect of any symbolic structure is indefinite, works of this kind cannot yield entirely to analysis. If, however, as some maintain, literature is increasingly private, reading it in company seems a good way to make it almost public again and all but sociable.

To convey the experience of reading such works, we commonly have recourse to the metaphor of levels. The work seems many-leveled like a cake, which, if eaten from the top down, reveals layer after layer of agreeable substance. Maybe, however, the metaphor owes no more to cake than to Dante's seven-story mountain or else to Freud's dream, in which the manifest content seems to occupy a level above the latent. Whether it owes its origin to cake, Freud, or Purgatory, the overworked metaphor is inexact; for everything a book contains is present or implicit on the printed page. There are no levels. The surface may be so difficult that we do not find at once what is there, but surface is all. Both Saint Thomas and Dante, considering the senses of a text, placed emphasis upon the literal, which must contain the others. Yet level, suggesting at least a third dimension, may do for our experience of deeper and deeper penetration if not for the work itself. As for that, we

From The Literary Symbol *by William York Tindall (New York: Columbia University Press, 1955), pp. 71–72. Copyright © 1955 by Columbia University Press. Reprinted by permission of the publisher.*

may change the metaphor for that of the symphony, which implies time, or for those of labyrinth or world, which imply surface, organization, and development. Whatever the trope, it means that, entering the work by degrees, we discover parts at first and, if we can, the whole; or else that, having felt the whole, we discover parts.

Though none of these tropes fits the great Victorian novels, some of them, displaying symbols, distantly anticipate the poetic novel of our day. The "London particular" that fills the first chapters of *Bleak House* is a case in point. Fixing the atmosphere through which the narrative gropes, this fog suggests Jarndyce and Jarndyce, a trial as incomprehensible and monstrous as something from Kafka; and when reappearing as "a dense particular" in the third chapter of *Finnegans Wake,* it suggests by allusion the kind of evidence, gossip, and slander that plagues H. C. Earwicker's trial. Mr. Krook's warehouse of rags, paper, bottles, and bones in *Bleak House* not only supports and expands the image of fog but, like the junk shops of Dickens's other novels, the heaps of "dust" that fill the back yard in *Our Mutual Friend,* and the dark, cobwebby room in *Great Expectations,* embodies feeling and thought about middle-class society.

Murray Krieger: *Bleak House* and *The Trial*

The greatest obstacle for the critic who would trace without a leap the movement in *The Trial* from the literal to the symbolic levels is Kafka's failure to relate in any workable way "the Court in the Palace of Justice" to "the one with the skylight" (*The Trial* by Franz Kafka, translated by Willa Muir and Edwin Muir, New York: Knopf, p. 131). K.'s use of these terms acknowledges the distinction, as does Huld's comparison between "an Advocate for ordinary legal rights and an Advocate for cases like these" (*The Trial,* p. 236). I am unable to do more than dodge this obstacle since I am unable to clear it. Here is the point where Kafka's aesthetic incompleteness shows, where the pure symbolist and the allegorist *manqué* struggle with each other inconclusively in the mist. How much more promising, for example, is the arrangement with which Dickens begins in *Bleak House,* where the legal court and the absurd court merge in the impossible actuality

"Bleak House *and* The Trial." *From* The Tragic Vision *by Murray Krieger (New York: Holt, Rinehart & Winston, Inc., 1960), pp. 138–40. Copyright © 1960 by Murray Krieger. Reprinted by permission of the publisher.*

of Chancery. The world of social-economic reality and of nightmarish fantasy, the political and metaphysical levels have a single narrative source full enough to sustain both at once. We feel the symbol of Chancery as Dickens creates it supports an equal sense of cogency on either level.

But this rooting of the symbolic level in the bedrock of a detailed social reality comes at a cost. For Rick Carstone, Chancery is more than just an oppressive social institution capable of reform; it is rather an unshakeable and suprahistorical curse upon the human condition. Totally irrational, bathed in the accretion of fogs of many generations, run by an enormous machinery of dehumanized creatures who justify what they cannot control, this monstrous collection of debris asserts itself upon the suitor before the court—born into the case or thrust into it—with the promise of a total resolution that it cannot help but frustrate and a bright future that it cannot help but blight. Its monumental absurdity that promises the clarity of order attracts irresistibly, feeds slowly and long, destroys utterly. It functions as this more than social evil, as this sphinx, for Rick, for Miss Flite, for Gridley, and for countless others, even as such symbols of the court as Krook and Mr. Tulkinghorn considerably exceed mere human dimensions. Yet there is in *Bleak House* another possible attitude toward the court, that of John Jarndyce, which can ensure freedom from it. Though a part of that great memorial of Chancery practice, Jarndyce and Jarndyce, by birth, "he has resolutely kept himself outside the circle" (Scribner's, 1897, II, 101). Unlike the others, he simply stays away from court and takes no interest. And it works, for he remains unaffected.

But is one free, once so totally involved, merely to wash his hands? Rick, once dragged in, insists that Chancery "taints everybody" (II, 101) with no possibility of exemption. To be born into an unsettled case is to be thrust into a senseless world that one must struggle to straighten out before the leisure of living can begin. And if the nature of the court precludes the chance of anything ever being settled, then the struggle is a desperate and ill-fated one but cannot be abandoned on that account. For one is not free to abandon it. Thus Chancery grows into a metaphysical entity reflecting the nature of existence as much as the legal tangles and abuses of Victorian England. But then along comes John Jarndyce to short-circuit this significance. Through the force of his virtuous will, though continually challenged he does stay outside successfully and does well to do so. All who follow him, like Esther and George Rouncewell, don his coat of invulnerability, finally manage what K. thought of as "a mode of living completely outside the jurisdiction of the Court," and with it manage a happy ending. A happier ending for all will come, presumably, when the court system is reformed.

Is the court an inevitable intrusion upon the human condition, then, or is it just an actual court and no more, one that can simply be ignored by the wise and changed by the well-meaning? It cannot be both as Dickens seems to make it. His difficulty may arise in large part from his rooting the court in reality. This raises the always delicate problem of creating symbolic levels without threatening the literal believability of the actuality from which they spring. Kafka evades the problem by postulating pure fantasy from the start, by separating his Court from the courts embedded in society. It is an easier way but a more troublesome and less satisfying one than Dickens' could have been had he resolved his problem more consistently. Of course, one must admit that these imperfections in *Bleak House* may not mean that Dickens could not resolve his technical problem so much as that he wanted to appease the tastes of Victorian readers and so inserted the sentimental story of Esther Summerson to compensate for the gloom and the terror of Rick's tragic involvement. Unfortunately, the serenely happy ending of the one totally reduced the immense capacities for vision in the other.

Taylor Stoehr: The Novel as Dream

The function of Lady Dedlock's self-control is to conceal her passionate nature. She is a woman who has broken the laws of her society in a wild love affair; she gives way to fits of rage and grief in the privacy of her boudoir. Only a strict constraint—imitative of the very laws she has broken—allows her to keep up the front of gentility she shows the world. Just as society and its laws by suppressing natural impulse and desire until they explode in unnatural violence, produce the spontaneous combustion that is the symbolic climax of the Chancery half of the novel, so in Lady Dedlock herself the pressure exerted by Tulkinghorn combined with her own characteristic restraint finally results in a murderous explosion of violence. For, in a reading of the

"The Novel as Dream." From Dickens: The Dreamer's Stance *by Taylor Stoehr (Ithaca, N.Y.: Cornell University Press, 1965), pp. 165–69. Copyright © 1965 by Cornell University. Reprinted by permission of the publisher.*

novel as dream, Lady Dedlock herself must be regarded as the murderess.

We have already seen how Lady Dedlock is a surrogate for Esther in the third-person narrative; similarly, Mademoiselle Hortense becomes the surrogate of Lady Dedlock in killing Tulkinghorn. Lady Dedlock has often wished him dead, and she is naturally suspected of the murder: "If she really were the murderess, [her horror and fear] could hardly be, for the moment, more intense" (LV). Typical dream devices connect her desire with Mademoiselle Hortense's act. They are lady and maid; each disguises herself in order to be mistaken for the other; each acts out of excessive pride, yet each finds herself a suppliant to Esther at some point in the novel (XXIII, XXXVI). Both hate Tulkinghorn, both visit his chambers on the fatal night, and so on. In the chief difference between the two lies a clue to the true meaning of the doubling: the violence Lady Dedlock has suppressed is fully embodied in Mademoiselle Hortense's character and action. Like Lady Dedlock, she also combines constraint and violence, as in her barefoot walk through the wet grass (XVIII); but the balance of passion is much higher in the complexion of the maid. Dickens' favorite image for her is that of a savage animal—she is called a "vixen" and a "tiger." It is she who acts out Lady Dedlock's deadly wishes, with the result that the deadlock of impulse and constraint suggested by her name is finally shattered:

> What was his death but the key-stone of a gloomy arch removed, and now the arch begins to fall in a thousand fragments, each crushing and mangling piecemeal! . . . The complication of her shame, her dread, remorse, and misery, overwhelms her at its height; and even her strength of self-reliance is overturned and whirled away, like a leaf before a mighty wind. (LV)

This final "key" image releases Lady Dedlock from the prison of her life of pretense. Tulkinghorn has represented the repressive and secretive aspects of her character, Mademoiselle Hortense the violence; the conflict between them results in the destruction of the restraint, and frees Lady Dedlock for her punishment and the expiation of her guilt. This is expressed by the plot, in Lady Dedlock's flight and death. It is also suggested by Mademoiselle Hortense's final speeches in justification of her own act:

> "Can you make a honourable lady of Her? . . . Or a haughty gentleman of *Him?* . . . You cannot do these things? Then you can do as you please with me." (LIV)

Mademoiselle Hortense's motives seem to have shifted now that the
murder is done. Whereas it appeared to be directed against Tulkinghorn (who had threatened her) it now seems to have been a means of
punishing Lady Dedlock. This inference corresponds almost exactly
with what would have been Lady Dedlock's motives for killing Tulkinghorn, *had* she done it herself:

> For as her murderous perspective, before the doing of the deed, however
> subtle the precautions for its commission, would have been closed up by
> a gigantic dilatation of the hateful figure, preventing her from seeing
> any consequences beyond it; and as those consequences would have
> rushed in, in an unimagined flood, the moment the figure was laid low—
> which always happens when a murder is done; so now she sees that when
> he used to be on the watch before her, and she used to think, "if some
> mortal stroke would but fall on this old man and take him from my
> way!" *it was but wishing that all he held against her in his hand might
> be flung to the winds, and chance-sown in many places.* (LV; my italics)

Like Carton and Darnay in *A Tale of Two Cities* or Wrayburn and
Headstone in *Our Mutual Friend,* Lady Dedlock and Mademoiselle
Hortense are symbolic twins, projections onto separate characters of
the conflicting impulses of the dreamer. Through them Dickens conveys the ambivalence and complexity of his dream meaning without
expressly stating it. The mystery of Tulkinghorn's murder thus has the
following place in the total configuration of sex, class, and violence:
Society, whose systematizing, delimiting, law-making aspects are represented by Tulkinghorn and the legal profession, enchains and represses
human nature, which nevertheless expresses itself in violations of these
laws (the crossing of class boundaries, the breaking of sexual mores);
the result is illegitimacy, guilt, and the need for deception and hypocrisy; finally the deception must be uncovered, the illegitimacy punished, the guilt expiated; and all this is accomplished when the repression—originally a cause of the crime, now a part of the guilt and the
attempt to hide it—becomes so constrictive that the system itself splits
open in an explosion of violence, representing both a return to nature
and impulse and also a punishment and atonement for the sin. This
pattern of repression and explosion may be seen again and again in
the novel—in the symbolic connections between Chancery and Krook's
spontaneous combustion, and in the stories of Tom Jarndyce and
Gridley, as well as in the main plot involving Lady Dedlock. Minor
exemplars of the same motif crop up everywhere: in the bars of the
gate to the burial ground where Nemo lies, in the numerous threats

and warnings, arrests and imprisonments, in the explosions of guns, the images of lightning flashing, floodgates opening, arches tumbling. In the symbolic weave of the hidden dream meaning, all these fragments repeat the larger pattern.

Again, these connections may be traced back to the blacking-warehouse experience and the jailing of Dickens' father for debt. No doubt it was during that time that the image of prison first grew large for Dickens as a sign of the forbidding and constraining forces of society, opposed to his own nature and freedom. But his novels do not merely reflect his own past, or even his judgment of the society of his day and its problems; their hidden content also provides a close analogue of the dream manner in his writing. The forces of order and repression in the stories are equivalent to the censorship and secondary elaboration which obscure and layer over the true meanings of his dreams, the impulses of fear and desire which, thus repressed, erupt throughout the novel in apparently unrelated scenes of violence like Krook's spontaneous combustion or Tulkinghorn's murder. Split narratives, doublings of characters, displacements of emotion and life from the characters into their surroundings—these all are comparable to the devices of dreamwork, at once concealing and revealing the meaning, just as the legalistic mores of society have cramped and distorted human beings into grotesques like Miss Flite and Krook, Phil Squod and Volumnia Dedlock, Mr. Turveydrop and Grandfather Smallweed, or like Tulkinghorn himself, who "dwelling among mankind but not consorting with them, aged without experience of genial youth, and so long used to make his cramped nest in holes and corners of human nature . . . has forgotten its broader and better range . . ." (XLII).

Chronology of Important Dates

Dickens	The Age
1812 Birth of Dickens, February 7th.	
1832	Passage of First Reform Act.
1836–37 Publication of *Pickwick Papers*; married, edited *Bentley's Miscellany*, began *Oliver Twist*.	
1837	Accession of Queen Victoria. Publication of Carlyle's *French Revolution*.
1842 First American reading tour.	Chartist riots. Passage of Ashley's Act abolishing woman and child labor in mines.
1843–44 Publication of *Martin Chuzzlewit*. Lived in Italy, 1844–45.	
1846	Potato famine in Ireland. Corn Laws repealed.
1847 Established Urania Cottage, a home for poor women.	Publication of Thackeray's *Vanity Fair*, C. Bronte's *Jane Eyre*, E. Bronte's *Wuthering Heights*.
1849–50 Publication of *David Copperfield*.	
1850 Became editor of *Household Words*.	Factory Act established 10½ hour workday. Tennyson's *In Memoriam* published.
1851	Great Exhibition. Passage of Chancery Reform Act.
1852–53 Publication of *Bleak House*.	
1854 *Hard Times* published in *Household Words*.	Crimean War.
1857	Indian Mutiny. Publication of Trollope's *Barchester Towers*.

1858	Separated from wife. Began public readings.	
1859	Became editor of *All the Year Round.*	Publication of *Origin of Species* by Darwin and George Eliot's *Adam Bede.*
1860–61	*Great Expectations* published in *All the Year Round.*	
1861		Death of Prince Albert.
1866		Hyde Park riots.
1867	Began second American tour.	Disraeli became Prime Minister. Passage of Second Reform Act.
1870	Farewell readings, January to March. Died of stroke, June 8th.	Elementary Education Act made elementary education universal.

Notes on the Editor and Contributors

JACOB KORG, Professor of English at the University of Washington, is Visiting Professor at the University of Maryland. He is the author of books on George Gissing and Dylan Thomas.

G. ARMOUR CRAIG has taught at Harvard, and is Professor of English at Amherst College.

LEONARD W. DEEN is a member of the Department of English at Queens College of the City University of New York.

ROBERT A. DONOVAN is Professor of English at the State University of New York at Albany. He is the author of studies of Matthew Arnold and Samuel Richardson's *Pamela*.

ROBERT E. GARIS is a member of the Department of English at Wellesley College. He has taught at Harvard and has held a Fulbright Fellowship in England.

EDGAR JOHNSON is Professor of English at the City College of the City University of New York. He is the author of numerous books and articles, and has edited *The Heart of Charles Dickens,* an important collection of Dickens' letters.

MURRAY KRIEGER is Professor of English at the University of California at Irvine. He is the author of *The New Apologists for Poetry* and *A Window to Criticism: Shakespeare's Sonnets and Modern Poetics*.

J. HILLIS MILLER is Professor of English at Johns Hopkins University. He is the author of *The Disappearance of God* and *Poets of Reality* and other studies of modern and nineteenth-century literature.

MARK SPILKA is Professor of English at Brown University. He is the author of *The Love Ethic of D. H. Lawrence* and other studies of modern literature.

TAYLOR STOEHR is a member of the Department of English at Cornell University. He is a graduate of the University of California at Berkeley.

WILLIAM YORK TINDALL is Professor of English at Columbia University. He is the author of numerous books and articles on modern literature, James Joyce, Dylan Thomas, and D. H. Lawrence. His publications include *The Literary Symbol* and *Forces in Modern British Literature*.

Selected Bibliography

Axton, William, "The Trouble with Esther," *Modern Language Quarterly,* XXVI (1965), 545–57. Accounts for Esther's apparent inconsistencies by showing her to be self-conscious and sensitive to her social position, but determined to overcome her disadvantages by achieving moral superiority.

Blount, Trevor, "Poor Jo, Education, and the Problem of Juvenile Delinquency in Dickens' Bleak House," *Modern Philology,* LXII (1965), 325–38. Discusses Jo in relation to Richard Carstone and other characters, presenting him as an expression of Dickens' views about the influence of environment on character.

Butt, John, and Kathleen Tillotson, "The Topicality of Bleak House," Chapter VII of *Dickens at Work.* London: Methuen & Co. Ltd., 1957. Relates the novel to the current problems with which it was concerned, giving much valuable factual information.

Ford, George, "Self-Help and the Helpless in Bleak House," in *From Jane Austen to Joseph Conrad,* eds. Robert C. Rathburn and Martin Steinmann, Jr. Minneapolis: University of Minnesota Press, 1958. Shows how the novel divides its characters into those who follow bourgeois principles and those who do not, and examines its treatment of moral responsibility.

Fradin, Joseph I., "Will and Society in *Bleak House,*" *PMLA,* LXXXI (1966), 95–109. A detailed examination of *Bleak House* as a "metaphor of the divided modern consciousness," which finds a place for nearly every significant character and event within its interpretation of the novel as a critique of the social will.

Harvey, W. J., "Chance and Design in *Bleak House,*" in *Dickens and the Twentieth Century,* eds. John Gross and Gabriel Pearson. London: Routledge & Kegan Paul Ltd., 1962. Examines the way in which the two narratives interact with each other to produce a "double vision," and argues that Dickens' use of coincidence is a meaningful reflection of his view of life.

Sucksmith, M. D., "Dickens at Work on *Bleak House,*" *Renaissance and Modern Studies,* IX (1965), 47–85. Publishes Dickens' memoranda and number plans for the novel in full with an introduction showing how they reveal the thought processes that entered into the planning of the novel.

Wilkinson, Ann Y., "*Bleak House*: From Faraday to Judgment Day," *English Literary History*, XXXIV (1967), 225–47. Suggests that a popular account of the combustion of a candle supplied Dickens with a metaphoric equivalent for the social system, and led him to present moral laws in *Bleak House* as counterparts of such laws of the physical universe as magnetic force, entropy, and conservation of energy.

Zabel, Morton D., "Introduction" to the Riverside Edition of *Bleak House*. Boston: Houghton-Mifflin Company, 1956. An exceptionally detailed and lively general discussion of *Bleak House,* containing many interesting comparisons with other novels and examining traditional and contemporary influences.

TWENTIETH CENTURY
INTERPRETATIONS

Maynard Mack, *Series Editor*
Yale University

NOW AVAILABLE
Collections of Critical Essays
ON

Adventures of Huckleberry Finn
All for Love
Arrowsmith
As You Like It
Bleak House
The Book of Job
The Castle
Dubliners
The Duchess of Malfi
Euripides' Alcestis
The Frogs
Sir Gawain and the Green Knight
Gray's Elegy
The Great Gatsby
Gulliver's Travels
Hamlet
Henry IV, Part Two
Henry V
The Iceman Cometh
Julius Caesar
Keats's Odes
Oedipus Rex
The Old Man and the Sea